A Casebook on Ken Kesey's
One Flew Over the Cuckoo's Nest

A Casebook on Ken Kesey's *One Flew Over the Cuckoo's Nest*

Edited by
George J. Searles

UNIVERSITY OF NEW MEXICO PRESS
Albuquerque

Library of Congress Cataloging-in-Publication Data

A Casebook on Ken Kesey's One flew over the cuckoo's nest / edited by
George J. Searles.
   p.   cm.
Includes bibliographical references and index.
ISBN 0–8263–1323–X
   1. Kesey, Ken. One flew over the cuckoo's nest. I. Searles, George J.
(George John), 1944– . II. Kesey, Ken. One flew over the cuckoo's nest.
PS3561.E6670533 1992
813'.54—dc20   91–30704
                                                   CIP

Design by Susan Gutnik.

to my sons,
Jonathan and Colin

Contents

Acknowledgments

This casebook could not have been completed without the help of a great many people. I am indebted first to the various scholars who have so graciously consented to my reprinting their work, and to the publishers of the journals and books in which these studies originally appeared. In addition, I must acknowledge the several tireless librarians—Raul Huerta, Bonnie J. Mitchell, Audrey B. Sotendahl, and JoAnne Werner—who provided invaluable bibliographic assistance. As in the past, I thank my excellent typist, Barbara Granato, and also my secretary, Kathy Kelly, who handled much of the paperwork connected with securing permissions and placing the manuscript. On a more personal note, I wish also to mention my uncle, the late John A. Kearney, who first taught me Kesey's truths, and my wife, Ellis, who helps me remember them.

Introduction

◆◆◆◆◆◆◆◆◆◆◆◆

George J. Searles

In its righteous anger, its rejection of authority, and its celebration of irrepressible nonconformity, Ken Kesey's *One Flew Over the Cuckoo's Nest* (1962) is certainly a book of its time. But it is, of course, much more than simply that. In addition to reflecting the brash, irreverent personality of the 1960s, the novel also develops a perennial theme of American literature: the struggle of a heroic (if flawed) individual in conflict with the status quo. Protagonist Randle Patrick McMurphy takes his place alongside Natty Bumppo, Huck Finn, *Catch-22*'s John Yossarian, and many others in a lengthy fictive procession of rough-hewn but sensitive outsiders at war with the leveling effects of societal norms and conventions.

The book's real importance derives more from its relationship to this longstanding tradition, and its purely artistic merits, than from its status within the countercultural canon. Despite its feel of almost spontaneous composition, *One Flew Over the Cuckoo's Nest* is exceptionally well-crafted, as even the most minor details function purposefully to realize Kesey's larger intentions. The novel is a masterpiece of symbolic orchestration, a stylistic tour de force, an outstanding instance of masterly authorial control. It is also an impressive example of literary daring and innovation, as Kesey's experimental treatment of narrative point of view, and his blending of realism and surrealism, invest the novel with an additional dimension.

Not surprisingly, the book is often assigned in college literature courses, and interest in Kesey's work remains widespread. Three book-length studies have appeared, along with a pamphlet, a Viking critical edition, two "special issues" of scholarly journals, and scores of articles. As a review of the annotated bibliography will reveal, academic critics have approached the novel from many directions.

1

Debate continues, for example, about the respective roles of McMurphy and Chief Bromden, the novel's schizophrenic Indian narrator. A number of critics argue that the Chief is at least as central a character as McMurphy. They base this reading on the idea that McMurphy is deeply tainted and the fact that the Chief grows in stature throughout the book, eventually achieving independence and emerging triumphant. Peter G. Beidler's essay "Ken Kesey's Indian Narrator: A Sweeping Stereotype?" and John W. Hunt's "Flying the Cuckoo's Nest: Kesey's Narrator as Norm" reflect this view.

Others, of course, maintain that McMurphy is the dominant figure, and cite as evidence his magnetism, his self-reliance, and his conscious decision to sacrifice his own well-being for the good of the other patients. Terence Martin's "*One Flew Over the Cuckoo's Nest* and the High Cost of Living" exemplifies this interpretation.

Appropriately, several commentators have explored the psychological dimensions of the novel, with respect both to its institutional setting and to the relationships among the characters. In "A Place Apart: The Historical Context of Kesey's Asylum," Robert Rosenwein suggests that Kesey's novel may have contributed to the trend toward deinstitutionalization of mental patients. In "Big Mama, Big Papa, and Little Sons in Ken Kesey's *One Flew Over the Cuckoo's Nest*," Ruth Sullivan notes that although the book disparages psychotherapy, Kesey makes effective use of the oedipal constellation to pattern the book's interpersonal tensions.

Another topic that has commanded the critics' attention is the function of myth in the novel. Among the most extensive treatments of this is Raymond M. Olderman's "The Grail Knight Arrives: Ken Kesey, *One Flew Over the Cuckoo's Nest*," which discusses Kesey's adaptation of the Wasteland/Grail Knight/Fisher King motif, and presents the novel as a modern fable of good versus evil, employing many traditional devices of American romance.

Symbolism, both secular and religious, is also a mainstay of this highly metaphoric work. Image patterns abound, as the book's mythic structure is everywhere supported by a complex undergirding of interlocking symbolic tropes. In his "Mechanistic and Totemistic Symbolization in Kesey's *One Flew Over the Cuckoo's Nest*," Don Kunz traces the many "nature-versus-machine" symbols, which constitute one of the main patterns. In his essay "Christ in the Cuckoo's Nest: or the Gospel According to Ken Kesey," Bruce E. Wallis elucidates the novel's

Biblical analogs, although he concludes that ultimately McMurphy is un-Christian, because motivated by self-centeredness and pride.

Some of the most interesting assessments of Kesey's art are those that liken him to other writers, especially Joseph Heller and Kurt Vonnegut. Two excellent discussions of these parallels are Jerome Klinkowitz's "McMurphy and Yossarian as Politicians," from his *The American Sixties: Imaginative Acts in a Decade of Change*, and James R. Tunnell's "Kesey and Vonnegut: Preachers of Redemption," which compares the two writers' moral convictions, asserting that each has contributed to our understanding of innate human dignity.

As with most works of any complexity, however, there have also been a number of negative responses to certain features of Kesey's novel, particularly its depiction of women. Certainly, a major theme in the book is that the patients have been emasculated by Miss Ratched (the overbearing ward nurse) and by other women in their lives. Richard D. Maxwell's "The Abdication of Masculinity in *One Flew Over the Cuckoo's Nest*" outlines this dynamic, arguing that the patients have collaborated in their own undoing. Maxwell embraces the conventional image of McMurphy as a charismatic hero who rescues the other patients from the castrating effects of matriarchal tyranny. Feminist critics, however, have adopted quite another view, charging that the book is a reactionary fantasy of male supremacy. Probably the most trenchant articulation of this position is Elizabeth McMahan's "The Big Nurse as Ratchet: Sexism in *One Flew Over the Cuckoo's Nest*." McMahan poses some probing questions and offers suggestions as to how this aspect of the novel might be handled in a literature class.

Other complaints have arisen in response to the 1975 film version, starring Jack Nicholson. A number of commentators—including Kesey himself, who has refused to view the movie—charge that director Milos Forman's rendering distorts the novel by diminishing the role of Chief Bromden and elimating the book's symbolic dimension. In relying more on realistic comedy and less on surrealistic metaphor, they say, the film retains the book's humor but loses its psychological depth. Elaine B. Safer's "'It's the Truth Even If It Didn't Happen': Ken Kesey's *One Flew Over the Cuckoo's Nest*" voices these objections quite succinctly. Other critics, though, have praised this hugely successful film, which won five Oscar Awards (Best Picture, Best Adapted Screenplay, Best Director, Best Actor, Best Actress). A particularly sophisticated appreciation, George B. MacDonald's "Control by Camera: Milos Forman as Subjective Narrator," explores Forman's use of color, and his variations on the subjective-camera technique. In a very different vein, the amusing *MAD* magazine satire by Dick DeBartolo and Mort Drucker warrants inclusion here as well.

Of Kesey's other volumes—*Sometimes a Great Notion* (1964), *Kesey's Garage Sale* (1973), *Demon Box* (1986), *Caverns* (1990, in collaboration with graduate students at the University of Oregon), *Little Tricker the Squirrel Meets Big Double the Bear* (1990), and *The Further Inquiry* (1990)—only the first has received much critical acclaim. But Kesey has been enshrined as a bohemian folk-hero, a role fostered in part by such accounts of his extraliterary escapades as Tom Wolfe's *The Electric Kool-Aid Acid Test* (1968) and Paul Perry and Ken Babbs's *On the Bus* (1990). And *One Flew Over the Cuckoo's Nest* has sold nearly eight million copies as of this writing. Surely, the book must be seen as one of the foremost American novels since midcentury, a work that will continue to repay close reading and study. This casebook, designed as a resource for students and teachers, is intended to facilitate that endeavor.

1
Ken Kesey's
Indian Narrator:
A Sweeping
Stereotype?

●●●●●●●●●●●●●●●

Peter G. Beidler

Tom Wolfe tells us that it was while Kesey was high on peyote that he got the "great inspiration" for having an American Indian as the first-person narrator of *One Flew Over the Cuckoo's Nest*.[1] We cannot be sure that Wolfe was right about the source or the circumstances of this inspiration, but clearly it was an inspiration for Kesey to choose Bromden as the character through whose eyes are seen, and through whose mind are analyzed, the other characters in the novel. To understand why this was an inspiration, let us consider the extent to which Kesey relied on familiar stereotypes of the American Indian in his characterization of Chief Bromden.

Let us note first some important facts about this paranoid schizophrenic. Bromden's father was an Indian chief, his mother a white woman. He grew up in an Indian village on the banks of the Columbia River in Oregon. When the U.S. government decided to build a hydroelectric dam on the Columbia River, the Indians were forced to accept a cash payment for their land, which was to be flooded behind the dam. As a result, Bromden's father lost his self-pride and eventually died an alcoholic, for the dam destroyed his people's village and their primary means of livelihood, salmon fishing. Young Brom-

Originally published in *Lex et Scientia: The International Journal of Law and Science* 13: 1–2 (1977), pp. 18–21. Reprinted by permission.

den seemed to adapt quickly to the white man's world. He grew up to be a very successful high school football player, partly because of his enormous size, six feet eight inches. After high school Bromden went on to college where he studied electronics. Then World War II came along, and after only a year in college he joined the Army, received training as an electrician's assistant, and was sent to Germany. Then Bromden's career as a successful white-style Indian halted, for he went crazy, apparently during an air raid on the military base. He lost his self-confidence, lost his orientation, lost his ability to function in the "real" world, and even lost his ability to remember who he was. When the primary action of the novel begins, Bromden, now in his early forties, has spent the last twenty years of his life on a mental ward in a state hospital in Oregon. Here he hides in closets and in an imaginary white fog when he needs to escape from whatever dangers, real and imagined, the ward presents. Because he spends most of his time sweeping the ward, he is known to his fellow patients as "Chief Broom."

Others have shown that Kesey relied on certain familiar stereotypes of males and females in creating certain of his characters. He also relied to some extent on familiar stereotypes of the American Indian in portraying Chief Broom. Take, for example, the stereotype of the Indian sidekick to the white leader. Chief Broom, like the Lone Ranger's Tonto and like Natty Bumppo's Chingachgook, is the loyal but rather uninventive Indian companion to McMurphy, the flamboyant white hero. Or consider the stereotype of the Indian as America's first ecologist and conservationist, the man who made wise and careful use of the earth's natural resources, who wasted nothing, and who did not leave a mess behind him. One small, possibly comic, but surely significant manifestation of this stereotype in Kesey's novel is that Chief Broom, whom one of the patients calls a giant "sweeping machine,"[2] spends most of his time cleaning up the dirt left in the ward. Another comic manifestation of it may be that as a "conservationist" he saves his used chewing gum for years by sticking it underneath his bed at night for recycling—that is, rechewing—another day.

Now, I have no quarrel with Kesey's use of stereotypes of the American Indian. It does not appear either that Kesey knew much about real Indians or that he wanted to say much about real Indians in his novel. He was writing fiction, not fact, art, not anthropology.

That is, he wanted to present meaning through carefully controlled characterization and action. If he could do that by means of selective and inventive use of stereotypes, so much the better. And while Kesey did base his characterization of Chief Broom on familiar images of the Indian, he both transcended those images and adapted them to his own artistic needs. I can best make clear what I mean by discussing in somewhat greater detail another of Kesey's uses of a familiar Indian stereotype, that of the Indian as innocent child who must be educated and improved by the Great White Father.

It is clear that McMurphy is a kind of father figure for Chief Broom. When McMurphy first breezes in from the penal farm, Chief Broom notices that he talks "a little the way Papa used to" (p. 16), and there can be no doubt that from that point on McMurphy is a second father for the Indian. Indeed, Kesey's story is the story of Chief Broom's second growth from babyhood to adulthood. The first growth had ended during World War II, when the Indian had gone berserk. Now, twenty years later, Chief Broom thinks of himself as tiny and weak. He is unable to talk, he must have all of his needs provided for by the hospital staff, and he is even tied into his bed at night so he will not fall out. On the first page of the novel, one of the black aides jokes that the enormous Indian will "mine me like a baby," and later, when an attendant turns off the light in the ward dorm that first night after McMurphy arrives, he says "Tha's right, babies, sleep tight" (p. 79). At least for Chief Broom, the mental ward is also a maternity ward, and it is no accident that a couple of the patients refer to the ward as a "nursery" (p. 107). In shaking Chief Broom's hand that morning, McMurphy had given him life and caused him to be reborn: "I remember the fingers were thick and strong closing over [my hand] . . . like he was transmitting his own blood into it" (p. 27).

McMurphy gradually brings his "baby" into each new phase of growth. It is to McMurphy that Broom speaks his first words in twenty years, the words "Thank you" (p. 185). It is McMurphy who offers in proper fatherly manner to take his "son" on a fishing trip. And it is for McMurphy that Chief Broom develops the physical strength to lift the heavy control panel. In short, McMurphy is the new father who re-engenders Chief Broom and who brings the helpless and confused Indian from babyhood to manhood. And at the end Chief Broom does what every normal adolescent does: after rejecting the mother (Big Nurse is sometimes called "Mother Ratched" by the patients) and murdering the father, he runs away from home. The murder of the father is in this case highly complex, for Chief Broom suffocates the recently lobotomized McMurphy in a murder that is at the same time an expression of his love for McMurphy, a demonstration of his revenge against Big Nurse, and an assertion of his independence from both. With his new-found manhood he then uses the four-hundred-pound control panel as a battering ram to smash through the window to freedom.

McMurphy, then, is clearly a "father" to this Indian child, but Kesey is not merely repeating in Chief Broom the familiar stereotype of the childlike Indian led into maturity by the morally and intellectually superior White Father. First, what we have here is really as much universal archetype as Indian stereotype. That is, Chief Broom's story is a variation on the archetypal rejection-of-the-parent motif, and not simply a variation on the Indian's acceptance of the White Father's leadership. Second, Kesey turns 180 degrees the direction of the White Father's influence. In most examples of the stereotype, the paternalistic White Father's job is to lead the primitive, uneducated, and unsophisticated Indian "forward" into the technologically superior culture of books, guns, machines, medicines, and televisions. In Kesey's novel we have the reverse of this movement, for McMurphy's paternalism is designed not to bring this Indian forward into the white man's world, but to take him back *out* of it, back to self-sufficiency and away from the corrupting influence of the white man's technological Combine. Third, this Indian's White Father may not even be essentially a white man, for in many ways McMurphy is more Indian than white. Unlike white men, McMurphy has not been significantly touched by the Combine. He has lived in or near a number of Indian communities. He is, as many Indians were before the white man came, essentially nomadic, for he drifts from place to place, refusing to settle down in any permanent home. And it is no accident, I believe, that some of McMurphy's friends nickname him "Red." He does of course have red hair, but he is also in essence an Indian or "red man."

So much for Kesey's use and transformation of the familiar stereotype of the Indian as innocent pupil to be educated by the White Father. Kesey both used and transformed another stereotyped image, that of the Indian as "natural man," the bronzed warrior standing with his bare feet on the warm and life-sustaining earth. Surely one of the reasons why Kesey wanted to have an Indian as the narrator of this story is that he wanted the action to be presented through the eyes and mind of a *natural* man. Chief Broom once stood outside of the technological Combine which so radically altered life in America. He represents that indigenous, close-to-nature culture which supposedly was here before Columbus and other Europeans came along and ruined it. Chief Broom can remember what the old ways were like before the hydroelectric dam was built and his village and its culture were destroyed. To the extent that he does remember, he is a useful literary device for Kesey because he has the perspective to measure the distance that the white technological culture has come from this more natural culture.

But, again, there is more to it that this in Kesey's novel, for this Indian is neither merely natural nor merely an Indian. For one thing, Chief Broom is an "insane" man, a paranoid schizophrenic who is incapable of taking care of himself in what the white man calls the "real" world. His incapacitating insanity, however, is also an aspect of his naturalness, for it is the technological Combine—the absolute antithesis of the natural—that is the primary cause of his schizophrenic disorientation and the primary object of his intense paranoia. If we consider his paranoia in more detail and ask what he is paranoid about, we find that he is afraid primarily of electronic and mechanical devices. He is afraid to go swimming because he is afraid he will go in over his head and "be sucked off down the drain and clean out to sea" (p. 147). He panics whenever the aides try to shave him with an electric razor. He is sure that a routine tuberculosis X-ray is really a subtle way of checking the circuits and machinery that the doctors and nurses have installed in all of the patients. He is sure there are electronic devices in all of the walls, and he is afraid to speak because he thinks there may be a microphone concealed in his broom handle. What he fears, in short, is the Combine—that huge, powerful, nationwide machine organization in which Big Nurse is a high-ranking official.

Now, there is no question that Chief Broom is insanely paranoid, for, literally speaking, there is no microphone in his broom handle, there is no huge drain in the swimming pool to suck him out to sea, and there is no nationally organized Combine with nefarious officers. These do not *really* exist. And yet, metaphorically or symbolically, they do. At the end of the first chapter of the novel, Chief Broom tells his readers that "you think the guy telling this is ranting and raving my *God:* you think this is too horrible to have really happened. . . . But it's the truth even if it didn't happen" (p. 13). Even if some of the things Chief Broom fears are literally impossible, he is still, in his own way, telling us something true about modern American life. Chief Broom, with that special vision of the insane and with that special perspective of a man with his roots in nature, feels that there is an enormous force that destroys the souls of men, that there is no longer any essential privacy in America, and that there is a vast social, political, and educational network dragging men away from love and honor down through a gigantic drainpipe into a polluted ocean. Chief Broom, the *natural* paranoid, expresses his fear in highly technological language. He sees modern man, with electronic circuits installed in him and his organs replaced by tubes, living in a world in which the "love" switch is turned off and the "rules" switch is turned on. His perspective is far more penetrating and far more complex than that of the stereotypical primitive, the noble savage, or the *mere* natural man.

Kesey made another crucial change in adapting the image of the Indian as natural man to his own uses. Usually the Indian as natural man is portrayed as a full-blooded Indian who has been thoroughly steeped only in the native way of life. Kesey made his Indian not the stock-in-trade, full-blooded red man, but a mixed blood. Perhaps the term *double blood* is more accurate in this case, for Chief Broom embodies both the remembered natural heritage of his Indian father and the more recent non-natural heritage of his white mother. He has been salmon fishing on the Columbia River, but also to college. He knows how to stalk a deer in the woods, but also how to wire an electric motor. His dual heritage lets him see with the eyes of a natural man who has come to understand how the Combine works, a natural man who has the intellectual ability and the technological training to understand the realities of contemporary life. Broom's father, the full-blooded Indian chief, had died a weak and miserable drunkard because he did not know *how* to fight back against the Combine. His mother, who was a full-blooded white woman, was so much a part of the Combine that she did not know that as a human being she *ought* to fight it. Only their son, who combines the natural with the technological, the red with the white, seems able to escape, with the fatherly guidance of McMurphy, from that insane asylum of life in modern America.

It was, then, an inspiration for Kesey to use an American Indian as the narrator of *One Flew Over the Cuckoo's Nest*. Through his artistically re-created stereotype of the American Indian in Chief Broom, Kesey was able to convey one of the central themes of the novel: the idea that most Americans have become robots, that the robots in America will probably destroy the *merely* natural men in the country, and that only the integrated man, the man who understands both the natural world and the technological world, can find the broom to sweep his way out of the trash of modern life.

Notes

1. Tom Wolfe, *The Electric Kool-Aid Acid Test* (New York: Bantam Books, 1969), pp. 42–44.

2. Ken Kesey, *One Flew Over the Cuckoo's Nest* (New York: New American Library, 1962), p. 65. All subsequent references are to this edition, and are parenthesized within the text.

2

Flying the Cuckoo's Nest: Kesey's Narrator as Norm

■■■■■■■■■■■■■■■■■

John W. Hunt

Initially the most striking feature of *One Flew Over the Cuckoo's Nest*, and, for understanding how the novel achieves its force and power, finally the most crucial one, is Kesey's use of Chief Bromden as narrator. In a remarkable thirteen-line paragraph ending the first short chapter, Bromden announces his subject as fear, his method as purgation, and his purpose as achieving the truth. The fear about which he will tell is his own. For twenty years it has been "burning down into him like steam," like the fear of a bluetick hound baying "out there in the fog, running scared and lost because he can't see" and picking up "no scent but his own fear." The story of this fear, he says, is "gonna roar out of me like floodwaters." And he is convinced that in some sense, which as he begins is still vague—"it's still hard for me to have a clear mind thinking on it"—his "finally telling about all this" will bring him to "the truth."[1]

Kesey's use of the single narrator who is telling a story deeply important to his own understanding of himself forces the reader to follow a double story line, one centering upon the tale told and the other upon the teller and the telling. In this and other respects Kesey's novel holds features in common with some earlier classics of American

Originally published in *Lex et Scientia: The International Journal of Law and Science* 13: 1–2 (1977), pp. 27–32. Reprinted by permission.

literature which implicitly pose for the reader the question "whose story is it?" Is *Moby-Dick*, for example, the story of Ahab or of Ishmael? Is *The Great Gatsby* Jay Gatsby's story or Nick Carraway's? Quentin Compson tells, and is told, Thomas Sutpen's story, but whose is the story in *Absalom, Absalom!?* One may establish that the story in each case is Ahab's or Gatsby's or Sutpen's, yet still he must give weight to the fact that their stories are what the narrators tell us they are. One should not press the question too far, of course, for as with all successful novels these novels are "about" many things, and they are finally, perhaps, too complex to yield a simple answer to so simple a question.

In Kesey's novel, however, though there is no lack of structural complexity, the narrator's story clearly dominates. Bromden's purgative act in "telling about all this, about the hospital, and her, and the guys—and about McMurphy" (p. 13), significantly comes in the shape of a story. That is, it comes in a form which requires that the events alluded to be ordered with a coherence sufficient to explain or yield their meanings to the narrator himself. Thus the story told is given its structure by the need of the narrator to find the truth in it, to understand what McMurphy's entry into the hospital ward meant for him. He organizes his recollections so that the events which transpire explain to him how he, Bromden, moved from being an incapacitated mental patient of twenty years' standing—feigning muteness and deafness and hiding in closets and in a protective mental fog— to a rejuvenated man at peace with his personal history and on the threshold of a greater degree of wholeness and freedom than he has ever known.

Normative in the novel, then, is the truth which the story of the hospital, and her, and the guys, and McMurphy yields *for Bromden.* Any novelist, of course, by the very act of projecting a fictional world, sets the limits and terms with reference to which the imagined facts of his story carry their meanings. But in *One Flew Over the Cuckoo's Nest* the truth attempted is of a special kind: it is a truth which generates its own facts. In all novels the reader is caught in an unavoidable solipsistic trap: the truth is only what the perceiving subject—whether the narrative point of view is single or multiple, inside or outside of the action, or a combination of different possibilities—allows it to be. But in Kesey's novel the narrator specifically eschews responsibility to ground his judgments in self-evident "fact." Rarely do novelists have their narrators risk their metaphysics so explicitly as does Chief Bromden.

In the remarkable paragraph ending the first chapter of *One Flew Over the Cuckoo's Nest*, Bromden warns that he will be telling us things we will think are "too horrible to have really happened . . . too awful to be the truth!" But "my *God* . . . please," he pleads, "it's the truth even if it didn't happen" (p. 13). He is insisting that answers to basic questions cannot hang upon so fragile a peg as "fact." He thus announces a highly sophisticated metaphysics in which reality supports "no brute, self-contained matters of fact, capable of being understood apart from interpretation as an element in a system."[2] His "system" is the story he tells, and his facts take on meanings fully understandable only with reference to the "system" of which they are elements.

In Kesey's novel, as in *Moby-Dick, The Great Gatsby*, and *Absalom, Absalom!*, the narrator seeks his truth by telling the story of a person of extraordinary stature who is flawed in an extraordinary way. The central figure is heroic, but by no means is he unambiguously victorious. He struggles against great odds, as heroes must, and loses, or at least dies, in the end. And he is, in context, a cripple, wounded by what he fights against. Ahab has literally lost a leg to the white whale, but the deepest wound is in his soul. Gatsby is crippled by a romantic notion of life in which the sounds of reality are drowned out by the jingle of money. "Can't repeat the past?" he cries near the end of the sixth chapter, "Why of course you can!" Sutpen's wound or weakness is what Quentin's grandfather correctly calls his "innocence," his incapacity to understand the primacy of love in the social setting he seeks to dominate. In Kesey's novel, McMurphy, as a psychopath supposedly flawed, receives his fatal wound when he abandons his psychopathic character and takes on a responsibility to right the wrongs done to others, with no motive of profit for himself.

Bromden's account of his hero is structured by the three phases of McMurphy's battle with Big Nurse: the first, ending with the television uprising scene; the second, with McMurphy's shattering the glass window of the nurses' station for the first time; and the last, with McMurphy's death and Bromden's escape. When he enters the novel on the "this morning" opening chapter 2, the protagonist of Bromden's tale is embarrassingly cliché TV-Western-American in his heroic posture, and he clearly identifies himself as such a hero. By the end of the novel he has achieved genuine heroic stature, at the price classically exacted for such an achievement. During the course of McMurphy's transformation and, Bromden feels, because of it, Bromden is slowly, with some relapses, lifted out of his fog into hope and freedom. As Bromden reports them, the crucial moments of McMurphy's transformation mark a path downward to tragedy and death, but for Bromden they concurrently mark a rise to cautious hope and life. These moments and their placement in the three phases of the tale told are worth looking at in some detail.

McMurphy comes onto the ward sounding big, laughing from simple self-confident joy, transmitting new "blood and power" (p. 27) in his handshake, just at the point when Bromden is emerging cautiously from one of his self-protective fogs. Bromden's impulse is to dive back into the fog, to let himself "go completely, . . . the way some of the other Chronics have" (p. 42). But this morning is different; at least "for the time being I'm interested in this new man—I want to see how he takes to the Group Meeting coming up" (p. 42). Many of McMurphy's surface qualities are attractive to six-foot-eight-inch Bromden because they remind him of his father and of what he might himself have become had not his personal history, especially the betrayal by his mother, reduced him in psychological size to the point of invisibility to others. But there is more to McMurphy than his surface: "the new guy *is* different, and the Acutes can see it, . . . different from anybody they ever met outside" (p. 83). Bromden defines the difference initially in terms meaningful in his private, paranoid world. McMurphy is free: he has never known defeat because "the Combine didn't get him" (p. 83). He is a new experience to Bromden because "he's out of control." "Maybe that's it," Bromden muses, "he never gave the Combine a chance [to install an electronic control mechanism] . . . because a moving target is hard to hit" (p. 84).

In fact, Bromden tries at all of the crucial moments of his growth toward wholeness to define what it is about McMurphy's person that distinguishes him as one who can cause such growth in others. It is not easy for him to define, not simply because he is limited by vocabulary and sensibility, but especially because McMurphy *is* a psychopath, and Bromden's protective paranoia is predicated upon his conviction that the psychopaths are in control both inside and outside of the hospital. Big Nurse, the manipulator, immediately spots McMurphy as "what we call a 'manipulator'" (p. 29). The only apparent difference between psychopath McMurphy and the others is that he is wearing hospital lettuce-green rather than hospital white or the colors of the Department of the Interior which took Bromden's father's land from him.

Bromden, of course, is not sophisticated enough to state the mystery in such a paradoxical form, but he does feel the full force of what is involved. During the television uprising scene which ends the first phase of McMurphy's struggle with Big Nurse, Bromden says his hand rose in support of McMurphy because "McMurphy's got hidden wires hooked to it." Then he admits: "No. That's not the truth. I lifted it myself" (p. 126). At another crucial moment later in the novel he struggles to identify the fact which contains the truth he is trying to understand. Just after he has broken the silence of at least ten years with a "Thank you" (p. 185) to McMurphy, he tells us:

> I wanted to reach over and touch the place where he was tattooed, to see if he was still alive. He's layin' awful quiet, I told myself, I ought to touch him to see if he's still alive. . . .
>
> That's a lie. I know he's still alive. That ain't the reason I want to touch him.
>
> I want to touch him because he's a man.
>
> That's a lie too. There's other men around. I could touch them.
>
> I want to touch him because I'm one of these queers!
>
> But that's a lie too. That's one fear hiding behind another. . . . I just want to touch him because he's who he is. (p. 188, first ellipsis in the original)

In both instances Bromden is growing, rejecting his paranoid rationalizations, and trying to earn his truth by facing it.

The truth that McMurphy ultimately holds for Bromden is available only if extrapolated from the total shape of the tale told. Unfortunately—and this is one of the weaknesses of the novel—once McMurphy makes the decision in full knowledge of the consequences to go ahead with his struggle with Big Nurse (chapter 8 of part 2), the Christ symbolism unobtrusively present in the tale before this moment becomes blatant: "be a fisher of men" (p. 198); "McMurphy led the twelve of us toward the ocean" (p. 203); "like there wasn't enough time left for something he had to do" (p. 218); "I wash my hands of the whole deal" (p. 232); "Is it finished? . . . Christ" (p. 271); and so on. But fortunately the Christ symbolism does not stand alone. The shape of the story is justified internally by the credibility of Bromden's growing self-knowledge leading toward his ultimate release to freedom.

At first McMurphy's wager that he can beat Big Nurse before the week is out goes well as he baits her and the aides, brushes his teeth with soap powder, flashes the Moby-Dick whales on his black undershorts, and uses the group therapy meetings to push for concessions. By manipulating Dr. Spivey, McMurphy has the tub room made into a game room. For a moment Bromden believes Big Nurse is beaten, but his despairing paranoid vision rescues him from optimism: "She's too big to be beaten . . . because she has all the power of the Combine behind her." The fog rolls in, and Bromden is "glad when it gets thick enough you're lost in it and can let go, and be safe again" (p. 101).

Incredibly, Bromden discovers, "McMurphy doesn't seem to know he's been fogged in" (p. 104). He tries to push through a vote to change the television schedule so the patients can watch the World Series, but fails. When McMurphy overreaches himself by failing on a wager that he can lift the four-hundred-pound control panel, Bromden goes deeply into the fog, and in the long last chapter of Part 1 his reverie includes images of faces and snatches of conversation from his childhood and Army pasts which buttress and reveal the depth of his paranoia. In his reverie Bromden aches for himself and for others, wishing that his fellow patients would crawl into the fog with him. But the reverie is interrupted as he becomes aware that McMurphy is talking in a group meeting, calling for another vote on the television–World Series issue. "He's still trying to pull people out of the fog," Bromden reports with irritation, "Why don't he leave me be?" (p. 123). When Big Nurse is thoroughly routed, shouting threats as the patients sit before the blank television screen, Bromden tells us, "there's no more fog any place" (p. 130).

A calm settles on Bromden's narrative now that "it's known she can be made to lose control" (p. 129): "There was times that week . . . I'd quit worrying about the Big Nurse and the Combine behind her" (pp. 139–40). The Combine is not gone from Bromden's mind, but it has become less threatening. He contemplates the mystery of his own personhood: "I'd take a look at my own self in the mirror and wonder how it was possible that anybody could manage such an enormous thing as being what he was." The fog machine has broken down, he speculates, and he begins "seeing lots of things different" (p. 140). In fact, he is able to see things—including his own objective physical self—for the first time in years. In an especially lyrical interlude, which becomes significant as a source of the imagery for the closing page of the novel, Bromden describes how he looks outside of the hospital window one night and actually notices the season. He also sees a dog, watches a V of Canada honkers cross the moon, and remembers lying by a campfire wrapped up in a blanket his grandmother had made. McMurphy has begun to give Bromden back the goodness of his past.

Just after the novel's midpoint, then, the end of the first phase of Bromden's tale leaves him in hope. From this point on, the pace quickens as Bromden grows stronger in accepting and understanding the enormity of being what he is, and McMurphy's character is deepened by his being forced to act out the consequences for the men on the ward of what he has become. The second phase begins when McMurphy learns that Big Nurse holds the ultimate weapon, the power to keep him permanently committed. He starts to conform in earnest, "polishing that latrine till it sparkled" (p. 149), and thereby betrays or causes the temporary collapse of each man closest to him: he stands idly by as Sefelt throws an epileptic fit; refuses to confirm for Harding that his wife, Vera, is a bitch; rejects Martini's need to have his hallucinatory visions confirmed as realities; and when he fails to support Cheswick's show of self-assertion in opposition to Big Nurse, Cheswick, despairing that even a McMurphy can't win, commits suicide. As McMurphy begins to conform, Bromden begins to "feel afraid" (p. 149). His language of paranoia is employed more often as he makes excuses for McMurphy: "He's finally getting cagey, is all. The way Papa finally did. . . . It's safe. Like hiding" (pp. 150–51). The fog machine is reactivated, for "whatever it was went haywire in the mechanism, they've just about got it fixed again" (p. 156).

During this second phase, Bromden notes that McMurphy begins to show signs of exhaustion, his face taking on a "haggard, puzzled look of pressure" (p. 155) since he is no longer sure who the enemy is. It's not Big Nurse: she is "just a bitter, icy-hearted old woman." "There's something bigger making all this mess," McMurphy tells the men, yet "he finally gives up when he can't explain it": "I tell you, man, I don't know. I never seen the beat of it." Paranoid Bromden, however, isn't confused. McMurphy is beginning to see things for what they are:

> *McMurphy doesn't know it, but he's onto what I realized*
> *a long time back, that it's not just the Big Nurse by*
> *herself, but it's the whole Combine, the nation-wide*
> *Combine that's the really big force, and the nurse is just*
> *a high-ranking official for them. (p. 165)*

When McMurphy learns that most patients on the ward are self-committed and could walk away anytime if they had the courage, his reaction is utter confusion, almost despair: "I don't seem able to get it straight in my mind" (p. 168).

In the last chapter of part 2, as the recognition scene triggers the denouement, the story told reaches a climax with the economy of classical tragedy and falls in a downward path across the rising story line of the teller himself. A ringing begins in Bromden's head, mounting in intensity as he watches McMurphy at a group meeting "sitting in his corner," not "fiddling with a deck of cards or dozing into a magazine like he had been during all the meetings the last two weeks," and not "slouched down," but "sitting up stiff in his chair with a flushed, reckless look on his face." Bromden waits, sensing the self-recognition that is coming, "scared it would happen, and . . . just a little scared it wouldn't" (p. 170). When McMurphy rises, stretches, yawns, scratches his nose, hikes up his pants, strolls across the dayroom floor toward Big Nurse sitting by the nurses' station, and runs his hand through the glass window as he reaches for some cigarettes, the ringing in Bromden's head stops: "He was the logger again, the swaggering gambler, the big redheaded brawling Irishman, the cowboy out of the TV set walking down the middle of the street to meet a dare" (p. 172). Later Bromden says, "it was bound to be." McMurphy had "signed on for the whole game" (p. 260). McMurphy had leapt into Ophelia's grave.

In the third phase of the tale told, McMurphy, the big, blustering man of Eros, becomes the frantic, destiny-driven but life-giving man of Agape. In a sense, his story is now over, for his new character has been formed, and left for Bromden to detail are only the specific circumstances which make up what was bound to be. The final events of McMurphy's life seem to the reader, as to Bromden, to lack vitality, to be characterized by fatigue and deliberateness, and our interest shifts to Bromden. McMurphy shatters the glass on the nurses' station for the second time, starts a basketball team, and organizes a fishing trip to be chaperoned by "two sweet old aunts from a little place outside of Oregon City" (p. 177) who actually turn out to be two "workin' shimmy dancers and hustlers I know from Portland" (p. 189). When, after the all-night party on the ward and the suicide of Billy Bibbit, like a "sane, willful, dogged man performing a hard duty that finally just had to be done" (p. 267), he attacks Big Nurse and is lobotomized. Bromden recognizes that McMurphy's story is finished and, in an act of love, finishes his life.

As McMurphy's fate spins itself out, Bromden's fortunes rise. He begins thinking about his past more and more. He identifies the time he first began acting as if he were deaf, and he rehearses in his mind the scenes of his mother's betrayal and the loss of the tribal lands. "I was kind of amazed that I'd remembered that. It was the first time in what seemed to me centuries that I'd been able to remember much about my childhood" (p. 182). He speaks his first words in years, and signs on for the fishing expedition. When the aides proffer a broom for him to sweep the hall, with a new sense of himself he turns around and walks away: "The hell with that. A man goin' fishing with two whores from Portland don't have to take that crap" (p. 191).

After the fishing trip, Bromden's faith in McMurphy falters when Big Nurse insinuates that McMurphy is simply exploiting his fellow patients for personal profit. In an act of atonement for his backsliding, throwing "being cagey" to the winds, he joins McMurphy in a fight to protect George from Big Nurse's black aides. When, as a consequence, both men are sent to Disturbed and then to electroshock, Bromden reaches his own turning point in the novel, the point past which he can only progress to sanity.

During the night spent on Disturbed, after a Japanese nurse has confirmed for Bromden that all nurses and all females are not like Big Nurse, a disturbed patient with yellow teeth awakens Bromden in the middle of the night with "Indian! Look me, look me!" For the first time Bromden is able to articulate the pain of McMurphy's responsibility, having for the moment had the same kind of impassioned dependence thrust upon him: "That face, just a yellow, starved need, come looming out of the dark in front of me, wanting things . . . asking things. I wondered how McMurphy slept" (p. 234, ellipsis in the original). At this point Bromden is freed from his obsession with McMurphy as a heroic figure substantially different from himself. He can now pursue his own destiny, working his way back to reality.

Under electroshock Bromden's habitual "AIR RAID" response is, with no conscious effort, replaced by reveries of childhood. He recalls one incident in which, while hunting pheasants, he rejects his father's advice and turns out to be right, and another incident in which, in complicity with his father, he rejects his mother's scorn for their "uncivilized" Indian behavior of eating ants. The first remembered scene points to Bromden's new ability to act on his own without reference to the surrogate father, McMurphy, while the second shows a further rejection of his white mother and Big Nurse. At the deepest moment of his reverie, in the novel's title passage, he reaches back for a new touchstone and finds an Indian woman. He is playing "Tingle Tingle Tangle Toes" (p. 239), a child's finger game, with his beloved grandmother. She is a person of wisdom, a carrier of culture, a figure of both nurture and nature. Even if one misses earlier clues in the novel, such as the episode with the black girl in the cotton mill, it is important to see that the narrator, whose story this novel is, finds at the recognition scene of his story a woman who is fully a person, not a stereotypical victim or victimizer. Images of her life, death, and burial, and her reburial in the Indian tradition, sustain him as he fights his way back through the fog and, for the first time, wins: "I worked at it. I'd never worked at coming out of it before. . . . I had them beat" (p. 241). His newly found confidence is confirmed in the final scene of the novel in which he smashes through a window grating with the four-hundred-pound control panel and starts back to recapture his life.

Bromden's telling of McMurphy's story thus functions as a vehicle for his reaching a truth about himself, a truth which releases him from sickness and promises to make him whole. If we look at each of the stories, Bromden's and McMurphy's, in the context of the other, we see an exchange of visions, a clash between the originally tragic view of Bromden, to which hope has been added, and the hopeful view of McMurphy, which became completely qualified by tragedy from the day he signed on for the whole game. Though each attenuates the vision of the other, Bromden's vision remains the larger. In making Bromden his narrator, Kesey not only provides a voice to tell the events of a hero's life and death, but also a point of view from which to judge the events narrated. The narrator's own story at once arises from and incorporates the story he tells. In doing so, the one transcends the other, finds its own touchstone, and achieves its own truth.

Notes

1. Ken Kesey, *One Flew Over the Cuckoo's Nest* (New York: New American Library, 1962), p. 13. All subsequent references are to this edition, and are parenthesized within the text.

2. A. N. Whitehead, *Process and Reality* (New York: The MacMillan Company, 1929), p. 21.

3

One Flew Over the Cuckoo's Nest and the High Cost of Living

◆◆◆◆◆◆◆◆◆◆◆◆◆◆◆

Terence Martin

When Randle Patrick McMurphy swaggers into the cuckoo's nest, brash, boisterous, with heels ringing off the floor "like horseshoes,"[1] he commands the full attention of a world held crazily together in the name of adjustment by weakness, fear, and emasculating authority. As Chief Bromden says, "he sounds big" (p. 10). When, six weeks later, he hitches up his Moby-Dick shorts for the final assault on the Big Nurse and walks across the floor so that "you could hear the iron in his bare heels ring sparks out of the tile" (p. 305), he dominates a world coming apart at the seams because of strength, courage, and emerging manhood. As Chief Bromden says (repeatedly)—he has made others big.

The early McMurphy has a primitive energy, the natural expression of his individualism. And, in the manner of the solitary hero, his freedom and expansiveness come from being unencumbered. He has "no wife wanting new linoleum. No relatives pulling at him with watery old eyes. No one to *care* about, which is what makes him free enough to be a good con man" (p. 89). The later McMurphy, however,

Originally published in *Modern Fiction Studies* 19: 1 (1973), pp. 43–55. Copyright 1973, Purdue Research Foundation, West Lafayette, IN 47097. Reprinted by permission.

is thoroughly encumbered with the shrunken men on the ward, committed to a desperate struggle for *their* manhood—even though, as the Chief sees, "the thing he was fighting, you couldn't whip it for good. All you could do was keep on whipping it, till you couldn't come out any more and somebody else had to take your place" (p. 303). That kind of a struggle, necessary, sacrificial, and fierce in its dedication, is what Ken Kesey dramatizes in *One Flew Over the Cuckoo's Nest* with an intensity of focus at once sanative and cleansing.

I

"We are victims of a matriarchy here" (p. 61), explains Harding to McMurphy: Doctor Spivey cannot fire the Big Nurse. The authority to hire and fire belongs to the supervisor of the hospital, a woman and an old friend of Miss Ratched's from Army days (the supervisor is anonymous, a virtual extension of the Big Nurse). It is McMurphy's first lesson in the ways of the madhouse. Women in the novel, one comes to see quickly, are powerful forces of control. They represent a sinister contemporary version of a feminist tradition in American literature that goes back, at least, to Dame Van Winkle and that percolates through the popular fiction of the nineteenth century in the form of domestic tyranny—as Helen Waite Papashvily has shown with her chapter "The Mutilation of the Male" in *All the Happy Endings* (1956). Given the highly charged vision of *One Flew Over the Cuckoo's Nest*, female authority becomes nondomestic, hard, insistently emasculating.

Not all of the women are cast in the mold of the Big Nurse. Harding's wife, for example, is a bitch of the first order, whose visit to the hospital shows us all what Harding must overcome in himself as a prerequisite to overcoming something in her. Her remarks are guaranteed to make Harding fall back on defenses whose very existence she scorns. His laugh is to her a "mousey little squeak." His lack of cigarettes means that he "never" has "enough." And the ambiguity of that remark becomes "I meant it any way you want to take it. I meant you don't have enough of nothing *period*" (p. 173). Mrs. Harding enters flirting with a black orderly. She leaves speaking of the boys with "the limp little wrists that flip so nice" (p. 174), who come by to inquire about her husband. The Chief completes the picture: "Harding asks her if it was only him that they were dropping around to see, and she says any man that drops around to see her flips more than his damned limp wrists" (p. 174). If her visit suggests how Harding came to be in the hospital, it spells out even more clearly why he is afraid to leave.

In a different way, Billy Bibbit's mother denies him the chance to become a man. A receptionist in the hospital, she is a neighbor and "dear personal friend" of the Big Nurse's; her hair "revolve[s] from blond to blue to black and back to blond again every few months" (p. 281). Billy, on a comfortable day, talks about looking for a wife and going to college. His mother tickles his ear with dandelion fluff and tells him he has "scads of time" left for such things. When Billy reminds her that he is thirty-one years old, she replies, "*Sweet*heart, do I look like the mother of a middle-aged man?" Again, the Chief has a final word: "She wrinkled her nose and opened her lips at him and made a kind of wet kissing sound in the air with her tongue, and I had to admit that she didn't look like a mother of any kind" (p. 281).

Chief Bromden, too, knows of female dominance. His Indian father took his white wife's name when they married and suffered a diminishment of self ever after. The father's name signified his size and capacity as a man—Tee Ah Millatoona, the-Pine-that-Stands-Tallest-on-the-Mountain. But the five-foot-nine-inch Mary Louise Bromden got bigger and bigger and came to be "twice his size." The father fought the Combine, which of itself would make him smaller, "till my mother made him too little to fight anymore and he gave up" (p. 208). The female reduced the male—the white reduced the Indian. The Chief has only to think of his parents to know the legacy of his people.

Only McMurphy stands outside such woman-power. His name, with its patronymic, identifies him as the son of Murphy, not of Mrs. Murphy. (At the outset, Miss Ratched attacks that identity by calling him McMurry; she would, if she could, deny him his father.) But even McMurphy has had to pass a test of manhood. He looks at his old home—after the fishing trip—and speaks of the precocious girl of nine who first took him to bed when he was ten. The youthful McMurphy felt that they were married or that they should, at least, announce their engagement. Whereupon the young semipro gave him her dress and waltzed home in her pants. Under cover of night

McMurphy threw the dress out the window where it caught, permanently, in a tree. She "taught me to love, bless her sweet ass" (p. 245), he remembers. From that point on he became the "dedicated lover"—rather than a man in petticoats. His latter-day companions, Candy and Sandy, function both to emphasize his manhood and to measure the progress of the patients toward regaining (or finding) theirs. Drawn from the stock pattern of the fun-loving, "good" whore, Candy and Sandy evoke attitudes of freedom and openness rather than of restraint and confinement. Whereas the Big Nurse would make men little, they would make men big.

Matriarchy in *One Flew Over the Cuckoo's Nest* comes, we see, to be expressed in various forms of female tyranny. It can sink Harding into the quicksands of inadequacy or make a Lilliputian of the Chief's giant father. But its primary force and motive is to make men be little boys, to make them (want to) adjust to a role wherein lies safety. On the Disturbed Ward after the bruising fight with the orderlies (fought to protect George Sorenson—whose patronymic affords him scant protection), Chief Bromden notes the appearance of the Big Nurse: she "talks with McMurphy, soft and patient, about the irresponsible thing he did, the childish thing, throwing a tantrum like a little boy— aren't you *ashamed?*" (p. 268). If McMurphy—she calls him "Randle" at this point—will see his behavior in her terms, he will not be punished. When she finds Billy Bibbit with Candy, she shatters his newfound sense of manhood by wondering how Billy's mother will take the news. Billy wilts immediately; stuttering once again, he disavows affection and friendship, and the Big Nurse leads him into the office, "stroking his bowed head and saying 'Poor little boy, poor little boy'" (p. 302). After which Billy commits suicide, unable to become a man and be jerked back to boyhood all in the space of a few hours.

At Miss Ratched's disposal are the three black orderlies (hired for their hatred), the Shock Shop, and the final measure of lobotomy. With their thermometer, their giant jar of vaseline, and their blood knowledge of rape and injustice, the orderlies make women out of men, just as the shock therapy machine turns men docile, and lobotomy converts even the most unruly into Fully Adjusted Products. These are weapons of terror, dedicated to the proposition that the best man is a good boy. It is small wonder that the patients on the ward seek the relative safety of boyhood and allow themselves to be ruled by stern or selfish nonmothers who, like cuckoo-birds, have no instinct for building nests of their own. The Chief has his fog, but they have no other place to hide.

In such a world McMurphy, the epitome of raw, unvarnished maleness, represents all the Big Nurse needs to control. As the contours of the narrative take form, the bigger-than-life McMurphy and the bigger-than-life Miss Ratched come to be opposed in every way. He is the stud, she the "ball-cutter"; he is the brawler, she the manufacturer of docility; he is the gambler, she the representative of the house where chance has no meaning.

II

The opposition between McMurphy and the Big Nurse goes to the very center of the novel, to the perception of Chief Bromden. Whenever the Big Nurse seems in indisputable control, the fog machine churns out its mist, scary, safe, and scary again. When McMurphy wins a skirmish, the fog disappears and the Chief sees *clearly*. Before the second vote on watching the World Series, the Big Nurse, in total command of the situation according to the Chief's vision, fogs up the ward "thicker than I ever seen it before" (p. 127). Billy Bibbit looks "like he's a mile off" and things, including the Chief, begin to float in the eerie mist: "I never seen it this thick before, thick to where I can't get down to the floor. . . . That's why I'm so scared" (p. 128). But when McMurphy gets his majority, when he lifts the Chief "out of the fog and into the open" for the twenty-first vote, the change is dramatic. Acting collectively, the men have voted to have a say about their lives; the Big Nurse has been unable to keep them from doing so. At that point, "there's no more fog anyplace" (p. 141).

As part of the Chief's mode of perception, the fog machine is a metaphor for tyranny, fear, and hiding which becomes literalized in his narrative. During his Army days, when air fields would be "fogged" by means of a compressor for purposes of secrecy and safety, fog machines had an objective reality in Chief Bromden's life. Even then, however, the experience was subjectively ambivalent: "You were safe from the enemy, but you were awfully alone" (p. 125). An association between machinery and a paralyzing of vision, however, dates from earlier in the Chief's life. As a high school football player, he visited a cotton mill in California. "The humming and clicking and rattling of people and machinery" put him in "a kind of dream"; it reminded him of the men in his tribe "who'd left the village in the last days to do work on the gravel crusher for the dam. The frenzied pattern, the faces hypnotized by routine. . . ." As he talks to a Negro girl he notices that her face looks blurred, "like there was a mist between me and her. It was the cotton fluff sifting from the air." The scene in the mill "all stuck with me and every once in a while something on the ward calls it to mind" (p. 38).

Machinery, made by the Combine for the benefit of people who choose to live under the Combine, drove Chief Bromden's people away from nature into a world not their own. ("Joey Fish-in-a-Barrel has twenty thousand dollars and three Cadillacs since the contract. And he can't drive none of them" [p. 273].) Machinery, associated with authority, with the ward, with Miss Ratched, represents all that brings people into line. Kesey, we may note, invokes the full meanings of words to enrich Chief Bromden's vision. *Dam* can signify *mother*— and the Indians worked on "the gravel crusher for the dam" (p. 36), suggesting, at least to McMurphy-like minds, an activity as emasculating as "ball-cutting" and perhaps even more painful. (A man who "hath his stones broken," the Book of Leviticus stipulated long ago [21:20], is disqualified from entering the priesthood.) The sound of *Ratched* is virtually indistinguishable from that of *ratchet*, with its associations of machinery and distaff. And *combine*, as Raymond M. Olderman points out, carries with it the idea of "a mechanism, a machine that threshes and levels."[2] The experience in the cotton mill mediates between the Chief's early days with his people and his paranoid existence on the ward; his life, cut into pieces by machinery, has a frightening coherence. But McMurphy stands visibly in opposition to the fabric of the Chief's perception. Consistently unaware of the fog, McMurphy "keeps trying to drag us . . . out in the open where we'd be easy to get at" (p. 123).

The strategy of literalizing metaphors, used by authors as different as Hawthorne and Ionesco, lends force and credence to the world the Chief sees and presents to us. The Big Nurse is an expert in "time control." On a bad day she slows down time so that the minutes freeze agonizingly on the clock; on a relatively good day she accelerates time so that the men whirl through a period they might otherwise enjoy. When Harding explains to McMurphy that they are rabbits and comically singles out two patients to play the role, "Billy Bibbit and Cheswick change into hunched-over white rabbits, right before my eyes" (p. 63). And the Chief, as we know, has become literally deaf and dumb to the world because the world has treated him *as if* he could not speak and could not hear.

The words *big* and *little* likewise take on special meaning because of the Chief's literalizing vision. When McMurphy first shakes hands with Chief Bromden,

> *the fingers were thick and strong closing over my own,*
> *and my hand commenced to feel peculiar and went to*
> *swelling up out there on my stick of an arm, like he was*
> *transmitting his own blood into it. It rang with blood*
> *and power. It blowed up near as big as his, I remember.*
> *(p. 24)*

And so at the beginning—at a time when the Chief is helpless and little in a chair—we have an anticipation of the end: McMurphy's vital power will flow into Chief Bromden and make him big, at a cost terribly high and terribly necessary.

III

In his essay "The Concept of Character in Fiction," William H. Gass remarks that "a character, first of all, is the noise of his name, and all the sounds and rhythms that proceed from him."[3] Even in this primary sense, McMurphy is quite a character. His name not only proclaims his paternity but suggests the brawling Irishman of fiction and fact. Moreover, the *sounds* of McMurphy pervade Kesey's novel— and we are all the more prepared to hear them because we have a narrator like Chief Bromden. As I noted earlier, the Chief hears McMurphy before he sees him, and he "sounds big." He comes into the ward laughing—"free and loud"; it is the first laugh the Chief has heard "in years." After the first group meeting, McMurphy himself comments that the patients are afraid to laugh. "I haven't heard a real laugh since I came through that door. . . . Man, when you lose your laugh you lose your *footing*" (p. 68). The next morning the sound of McMurphy singing booms out of the latrine, and "everybody's thunderstruck." They haven't heard such a thing in years, not on this ward" (p. 88).

31

The Big Nurse's ward has its own sounds, among them those of canned music played loudly over a speaker throughout the day. Annoyed because poker bets can hardly be heard, McMurphy objects, and if we can credit his remark we can see why: "Can't you even ease down on the volume?" he asks the Big Nurse; "It ain't like the whole state of Oregon needed to hear Lawrence Welk play 'Tea for Two' three times every hour, all day long!" (p. 102). The consequence of his objection is that he gets another room for their game; the issue of sounds has resulted in more space for McMurphy's activities.

McMurphy's laughter and singing, his tall biographical tales, and the authentic ring of his idiom at once dominate the ward and define him to the other patients. His example, of course, evokes the choked-off manhood of the men on the ward and a sense of freedom they have forgotten, or not known. When, later, McMurphy organizes the fishing expedition, it is a shared adventure, exciting, fun, and noisy. During one hectic, scrambling moment on the boat, with Candy's breast bruised and bleeding and the Chief's thumb smarting red from the line, McMurphy looks on and laughs—"because he knows you have to laugh at the things that hurt you just to keep yourself in balance, just to keep the world from running you plumb crazy. He knows there's a painful side . . . but he won't let the pain blot out the humor no more'n he'll let the humor blot out the pain" (p. 238). Harding is laughing this time, and Scanlon, too, "at their own selves as well as at the rest of us." And Candy laughs, "and Sefelt and the doctor and all." The laughter

> started slow and pumped itself full, swelling the men
> bigger and bigger. I watched, part of them, laughing with
> them—and somehow not with them. I was off the boat,
> blown up off the water and skating the wind with those
> black birds, high above myself, and I could look down and
> see myself and the rest of the guys, see the boat rocking
> there in the middle of those diving birds, see McMurphy
> surrounded by his dozen people, and watch them, us,
> swinging a laughter that rang out on the water in ever-
> widening circles, farther and farther, until it crashed up
> on beaches all over the coast, on beaches all over all
> coasts, in wave after wave after wave. (p. 238)

Community laughter this, comic, aware, the signature of a deep experience, the expression of freedom—earned and shared. The fishing expedition, brilliantly handled by Kesey, accentuates the growing sense of community among the patients. It also contains the most joyous sounds in the novel. McMurphy, we know, has red hair, tattoos, and hands that bear the marks of work and combat. But his capacity for laughter is fundamental to his identity as a character—along with his ability to make us laugh. "That's clean enough," he says to the orderly watching him clean the urinals, "maybe not clean enough for some people, but myself I plan to piss in 'em, not eat lunch out of 'em" (p. 151).

The McMurphy who shakes hands with all of the men and announces himself as "bull goose looney" has much to learn about his new situation beyond the fact of matriarchal authority. He is, at first, what he has always been—the con man, the gambler in search of new territory—and he has managed to get himself committed to avoid the regimen of the work farm. Characteristically, he seizes the opportunity to bet on his ability to outmaneuver the Big Nurse. Surprised and disappointed when the patients do not support his motion to watch the World Series on TV, McMurphy again bets on himself, this time with a new purpose: his failure to lift the steel and cement control panel, foredoomed, according to the Chief, is an example of courage not lost upon the others. The next day they attempt the impossible and, as we have seen, reach their majority, twenty-one, in a second vote on the Series. (Interestingly, one of McMurphy's favorite games is blackjack, or twenty-one. Another, fittingly, is stud poker.) That they sit watching a blank screen, courtesy of Miss Ratched, gives their gesture an added, self-contained significance; the cowboy-hero turned home-run hitter is now in their midst. They are now, as even the Big Nurse knows, a different group from the one they were before the advent of McMurphy.

McMurphy goes through two other stages in the course of the novel, both the result of increasing awareness. From the lifeguard at the swimming pool he learns the difference between being *sentenced* and being *committed*. He realizes for the first time that he will be released only when the Big Nurse approves a release for him. The information has an immediate effect. As they are leaving the pool, a hydrocephalic patient from another ward lies helplessly on his side in the footbath, his head bobbing around in the disinfectant. Harding twice asks McMurphy to help him and Cheswick lift the boy up. "Let him lay," says McMurphy, as he walks on, "maybe he don't like deep water" (p. 163). The next morning McMurphy polishes the latrine "till it sparkled" and waxes the hall floors when asked to.

As the others recognize, McMurphy is playing the game, playing it safe—"getting cagey," the way "Papa finally did." At one time the Chief's father used to poke fun at the government men, speaking to them deadpan like a stage Indian addressing tourists—to the great amusement of his Council. Like McMurphy, Chief Bromden's father learned to play it smart. The other patients on the ward understand about McMurphy; they are not angry or even disappointed. But there is a fearful cost to McMurphy's decision to think of Number One: Cheswick, who has achieved a certain momentum toward manhood, gets caught in the drain the next time they are at the swimming pool and drowns well before McMurphy, the lifeguard, and the orderlies can bring him to the surface.

McMurphy has one staggering fact left to learn. It astonishes him into meditative silence, then catapults him into his final role of savior. He hears from Harding that only a few of the patients on the ward, indeed, in the whole hospital, are committed. The great majority are there voluntarily, because, as Billy Bibbit says sobbingly, they don't have the guts to be Outside. The news is hardly credible to McMurphy. But his reaction to it is swift and thorough. At the ensuing group meeting he walks "big as a house" toward the Big Nurse, the "iron in his boot heels" cracking "lightning out of the tile" (p. 189) and rams his hand through the window in the front of her office as he reaches for his cigarettes. When a new glass is installed, he does it again. And when a third glass is put in, with a whitewashed X on it to make it clearly visible, Scanlon accidentally bounces a basketball through it before the whitewash is even dry.

Direct violations of the Big Nurse's private office, symbolic sexual assaults, are only the beginning. McMurphy, aware now of what *committed* means, aware, too, that the frightened men on the ward are there voluntarily, and aware, further, that he cannot defeat the Big Nurse and all that is behind her—even as he could not lift the control panel—begins to act for the others rather than for himself. Before McMurphy arrived, the patients were set against each other in the name of therapy and adjustment. Each man was a spy for the Big Nurse, eager to write down information about someone else in the log book near the nurses' station. In group therapy sessions they would peck at the victim of the day, currying favor by making one of their own miserable. McMurphy once says (apropos of the way in which Harding and his wife make each other impossible), "All I know is this: nobody's very big in the first place, and it looks to me like everybody spends their whole life tearing everybody else down" (p. 174). It is a central insight for the unsophisticated McMurphy—and one of the truest and most generally applicable statements in the novel.

During McMurphy's final stage, things on the ward *begin* to change radically. Kesey, in masterful control of the fully activated materials in his novel, takes his madhouse men one last inevitable step, to an achieved sense of community. It is something he has consistently held dear: Ken Babbs's "great statement," Kesey remarked in an interview in *Rolling Stone* (7 March 1970), was—"'We don't want a commune, we want a community'" (p. 29). Kesey's "great statement," made eight years before, was to turn a bunch of rabbits into a community of men, "close-knit," as Joseph J. Waldmeir observes, and "functioning."[4] McMurphy organizes a ward basketball team, with Doctor Spivey (to Miss Ratched's amazement) approving—a team fated to lose its game against the orderlies, but a team, nevertheless, composed of people playing together in a common effort. The fishing trip deepens and enlarges the sense of community; as Raymond M. Olderman points out, it likewise evokes the idea of fertility and functions as "the central incident in McMurphy's challenge to the waste land"[5] of the hospital. And the party on the ward turns the great cast of characters into a group of Merry Pranksters, contributing, one and all, to a night of spectacular celebration.

The men on the fishing trip and at the party are a far cry from the little boys who spied on each other and tattled in the Big Nurse's log book. No longer do they *tear* each other down. Before Harding signs out and is picked up by his wife, *he* deals blackjack in the tub room and tells the silent Big Nurse on her return, "Lady, I think you're full of so much bullshit" (p. 307). The language of the novel virtually insists that we see McMurphy as a kind of Christ figure (at shock therapy time: "Do I get a crown of thorns?" [p. 270] and earlier: "McMurphy led the twelve of us toward the ocean" [p. 277]), doling out his life so that others may live. The action of the novel dramatizes the manner in which he makes his sacrifices, amid doubts and rejoicings on the part of his followers. And the perception of Chief

Bromden, now highly sensitized to the task, prepares us at times tenderly to appreciate McMurphy's legacy—manhood, friendship suffused with affection, and, finally, love. Miss Ratched's face at the time of McMurphy's last attack displays a "terror forever ruining any other look she might ever try to use again" (p. 305). She has her revenge, lobotomy, a "castration of the frontal lobes." But Chief Bromden denies the Big Nurse her trophy. "He creeps into the bed of his friend," in the words of Leslie A. Fiedler, "for what turns out to be an embrace—for only in a caricature of the act of love can he manage to kill him."[6] It is, of course, as Mr. Fiedler signifies, a true act of love, performed with a manhood McMurphy has poured into the Chief.

In the terms of the narrative, there can be no more fog or time control. Thus, the Chief, bigger than ever before, makes his escape by picking up the control panel McMurphy could not even budge— the epitome of all the machinery in the hospital, of all machinery that has victimized him and diminished his people ("I heard the wires and connections tearing out of the floor")—and throws it through the window. "The glass splashed out in the moon, like bright cold water baptizing [and thus perhaps awakening] the sleeping earth" (p. 310).

IV

Despite the fact that the term *Big Nurse* inevitably recalls the term *Big Brother* and thus invokes memories of *1984* and other controlled worlds, *One Flew Over the Cuckoo's Nest* is not, in its thrust and emphasis, an anti-Utopian novel. The specific make-up of the Combine remains vague, as indeed it must, since the word *combine* is not simply a synonym for *organization*, since it is the Chief's protean metaphor for all that mechanizes, threshes, and levels—for all that packages human beings into "products." In this sense, the idea of a Combine contributes powerfully to the dramatic coherence of the novel. The ward, the Chief says, employing the logic of the metaphor, "is a factory for the Combine. It's for fixing up mistakes made in the neighborhoods and in the schools and in the churches" (p. 38). The metaphor is not monolithic; there are other wards in the hospital. The Japanese nurse on the Disturbed Ward is pleasant—she gives gum to the Chief (a fresh stick), a cigarette to McMurphy, and she even criticizes the Big Nurse. And there is an Outside, increasingly regulated by the Combine, as is everything else, though not so rigorously as in the factory-ward.

On the trip to the ocean, Chief Bromden notices "signs of what the Combine had accomplished since I was last through this country": five thousand houses "punched out identical by a machine," five thousand identically dressed kids playing on an acre of "crushed gravel," five thousand men deposited like insets by a commuter train (p. 228). It is, recognizably, the world of our suburbs and subdivisions, standardized, mechanized, virtually anesthetized. Coming back from the ocean, however, the Chief

> *noticed vaguely that I was getting so's I could see some*
> *good in the life around me. McMurphy was teaching me.*
> *I was feeling better than I remembered feeling since I was*
> *a kid, when everything was good and the land was still*
> *singing kids' poetry to me. (p. 243)*

Again the Chief faces a world of threshed-out sameness; but he brings to it now—after the fishing trip—a sense of possibility which enlarges the dimensions of his spirit. The Combine, of course, continues to adjust things. But things may be increasingly adjusted (to pick up another idea from Mr. Olderman, who got it from McMurphy) because they are increasingly adjustable—which means, we realize with a sinking feeling of responsibility, that the Combine's power to control may exist in ratio to our willingness to forfeit manhood.

One Flew Over the Cuckoo's Nest directs our attention to such a point: we have surrendered a sense of self—which, for Kesey, is involved with a sense of space—and thus possibility. "The American has a sense of something that the European doesn't have," he remarked in the *Rolling Stone* interview, "and it's a sense of space. No matter how tight things get, there's more space, there's places you can go. . . . It's the most that we have to offer the world, just to communicate that sense" (p. 30). To lose the *sense* of space is to be confined (whether it be on the Outside or on the Big Nurse's ward), to contribute to the encroaching power of the Combine.

And so Kesey gives us McMurphy, the advocate of our manhood, who brings a sense of space, freedom, and largeness onto the ward as something coexistent with his life. We hear him, we see him, and once we smell him—the outdoor odor of man working. We are even treated on occasion to the splendor of his white-whale shorts. Given to him by a coed at Oregon State who told him he was a symbol, McMurphy's shorts have, no doubt, a sexual significance. If Melville can spell *archbishopric* with a final *k*, Kesey can surely play on the name Moby-*Dick*. Beyond that, McMurphy's shorts have already become ambiguous. Joseph J. Waldemeir, in his fine essay on Joseph Heller and Kesey, comes to see McMurphy as Captain Ahab because of his shorts.[7] And that, I believe, is an error with unfortunate implications. McMurphy may represent the indomitableness of Moby-Dick himself; as Moby-Dick cannot be vanquished by the monomaniac Ahab, so the spirit of McMurphy cannot be quenched by the Combine. Much more meaningfully, however, the leaping white whales suggest *Moby-Dick*, a novel that dramatizes with a fierceness of its own the interdependence of man in the face of Ahab's will to stand alone. Ahab curses the "interindebtedness" of man, that which binds one man to another; Ishmael sees it and accepts it, most notably, perhaps, when a literal line ties him to Queequeg in the "Monkey-Rope" chapter. And *Moby-Dick* validates Ishmael's vision of reality in the world.

The men on the Big Nurse's ward become stronger once they recognize their interdependence. McMurphy becomes heroic once he throws his lines out to them. And we come to appreciate the force of Kesey's novel once we see that *One Flew Over the Cuckoo's Nest* is an intense statement about the high cost of living—which we must be *big* enough to afford. That, I should think, is the "truth" the Chief speaks about at the outset. It will "burn" him to tell about it; it will "roar out" of him "like floodwaters." And it will remain true, for him and for all of us, "even though it didn't happen" (p. 8).

Notes

1. Ken Kesey, *One Flew Over the Cuckoo's Nest* (New York: Compass Book Edition, Viking Press, 1962), p. 10. Subsequent references to this edition will appear in the text.

2. Raymond M. Olderman, *Beyond the Waste Land: A Study of the American Novel in the Nineteen-Sixties* (New Haven and London: Yale University Press, 1972), p. 37.

3. William H. Gass, *Fiction and the Figures of Life* (New York: Vintage Books, 1972), p. 49

4. Joseph J. Waldmeir, "Two Novelists of the Absurd: Heller and Kesey," *Wisconsin Studies in Contemporary Literature* 5 (1964), p. 198.

5. Olderman, *Beyond the Waste Land,* p. 45

6. Leslie A. Fiedler, *The Return of the Vanishing American* (New York: Stein and Day, 1968), p. 182.

7. Waldmeir, "Two Novelists of the Absurd," p. 203.

4

A Place Apart:
The Historical
Context of
Kesey's Asylum

●●●●●●●●●●●●●●●●

Robert E. Rosenwein

As readers of Kesey's novel, we are accustomed to thinking of insanity as a form of sickness, as a form of "mental illness" which should be dealt with in the medical model, with diagnosis, treatment, and eventual cure. We see it as quite natural that the mentally ill should be isolated in places called "hospitals" where they can be taken care of. Most of us do not realize that this method of dealing with the insane is a rather recent one. The medical model of treating the insane did not come into being until the late 1880s, while the practice of institutionalizing the insane originated only fifty or sixty years earlier. Neither do most of us who read Kesey's novel realize that the last decade has seen an accelerating trend away from institutionalizing the insane and a profound questioning of the medical model itself.[1]

Moreover, we are conditioned by the medical model to focus on the individual and to view his insanity as a personal problem, one which needs to be solved or cured. It is often more difficult to see that insanity, in behavioral terms, is a socially defined form of deviance. Insanity is a label which different societies affix to different kinds of behavior. In fact the same behavioral manifestations, such as hal-

Originally published in *Lex et Scientia: The International Journal of Law and Science* 13: 1–2 (1977), pp. 34–37. Reprinted by permission.

lucinations or talking gibberish, may in different societies (or even in the same society but in different contexts) be defined quite differently. For example, hallucination may be seen either as psychosis or religious insight. Treatment, then, is not only a way of helping people in trouble, but also a form of *social control*, of dealing with actual or potentially disruptive behavior.

Viewing insanity as a social phenomenon having social meaning invites us to look at the asylum (the generic term to be used here) in Kesey's *One Flew Over the Cuckoo's Nest* as the outgrowth of a complex historical process in our society. Many of the practices and philosophies articulated by the staff in the novel are restatements of attitudes that originally led to the incarceration of the insane in asylums of the type described in the book.

In Western Europe, the practice of confining the insane in large establishments began in France during the late seventeenth and early eighteenth centuries, as part of a general social strategy to deal with the homeless and jobless masses who were beginning to fill up the cities. The insane found themselves in such places not because of any special qualities, but because they shared a general characteristic—unemployment—with many other casualties of economic crisis. Curiously, this practice had the effect of focusing attention on insanity as a special social problem for the first time. Prior to this and, indeed, back as far as we have records in Western history, the insane were usually allowed to roam freely among the general population. Although they were often considered possessed by evil spirits or potentially dangerous, the usual solution was to expel them forcibly from the bounds of a particular area, or systematically to ship or send them to some other location (the "ship of fools" in medieval iconography was indeed a real phenomenon of early times). With the confining of the insane, the fact of insanity became associated with the moral violation inherent in lack of employment, specifically, the violation of the work ethic, which equated sloth and social uselessness with unemployment.

Several forces conspired, during the mid eighteenth century, to separate the insane from other social deviants. Prisoners, the indigent, the unemployed—all were adamant in their objections to being forced to live with the insane. The administrators of the places of confinement complained that their attempts to establish workshops were disrupted by the unpredictable and confusing behavior of the insane. Many persons both in and outside the establishment were shocked at the "cruelty" of forcing anyone to live in close proximity to the insane. Finally, many persons were appalled by what was increasingly seen as the inhuman manner in which the insane were treated.

It is recorded as an important turning point in the history of European culture that Pinel and Tukes, two philosophers who were also medical doctors at the time of the French Revolution, separated the insane from persons in other low-status social categories and confined them in places for special treatment. But it must be understood that Pinel and Tukes shared the perception that insanity was a form of moral deviance. The behavior of the mad person, they thought, was a kind of moral marker. Such behavior staked out the boundaries of what was morally right as distinguished from what was morally wrong. The job of the psychiatrist-alienist-superintendent was to bring the mad person back inside the boundaries of the community, to make him aware of the burden of guilt he carried, to make him aware of himself as a free and responsible person—in short, to return him to the "rule of reason." The institutionalization of the insane became essential to this therapeutic enterprise, since incarceration allowed the director-therapist to exercise complete control over the welfare and behavior of the inmate. The confinement of the insane, then, became a much more explicit strategy for social control, and the goal was the resocialization of the insane person to the accepted moral norms of the community.

A similar evolution in the treatment of the insane is evident in American society. During colonial times—from the settlement of the colonies through the early eighteenth century—both the insane and the destitute were "cared for" by relatives or neighbors. Incarceration, even for serious crimes, was relatively rare. Instead, criminals were whipped, fined, put in stocks for a period, or branded. Beginning in the late 1820s, and especially during the 1830s, incarceration became the rule rather than the exception for all categories of social deviants. The reasons for this are complex. The rise of a new egalitarian ethic, the freedom—represented by frontier life and to some extent by Jacksonian life—to rise above one's station, to redefine one's social position, to "dream the impossible dream" was seen by influential men of the times as a serious and potentially dangerous threat to a social order in which everyone "knew his place." The causes of insanity were seen to lie in the evolution of modern civilization and its "discontents." The solution was obvious: remove the insane from the stress and strains of modern life to a place where an orderly and stable environment could be provided, and where a lesson in the proper way of living could be taught. It is no accident that the superintendents of asylums of the time were often educators and men of religion.

Another influence making itself felt during this period also led to the incarceration of the insane. The increasing complexity of social life and the increasing population, especially in the cities of eastern America, made the presence of the insane disruptive and disturbing. Having the insane "out of sight, out of mind" was perceived as an increasing necessity, both socially and psychologically. An outgrowth of this influence was the trend toward locating asylums away from centers of population, in isolated, rural areas. The therapeutic rationalization for this was that the insane should be in the more healthful, pacific environment of the rural countryside, rather than the stressful environment of the city.

It was not until the late 1880s, with the rise of the organized medical community, and with the discrediting of the philosophy of the early asylum superintendents, that the asylum became known as a "hospital" where the insane were to undergo a "medical treatment." Under the influence of the medical model, and encouraged by the success of physical treatment procedures, asylums came to be places run by doctors and staffed by nurses and therapists dedicated to curing an imbalance in the psychological state of the patient. At first, these treatments were almost entirely physical, depending in large measure on either shock (immersion in water, severe physical confinement) or relaxation. In the early part of the twentieth century, the influence of Freudian psychology and psychoanalysis began to be felt, and hypnosis and other forms of "talking therapy" were introduced.

In an important way, however, early rationales for the incarceration of the insane still persisted, and still do persist. Understanding them helps us to understand much of what happens to the patients in Kesey's novel.

One of these rationales was that moral resocialization was important in mental rehabilitation. An early idea about the function of the asylum was that it took men who had "fallen from grace," gave them back a feeling of social responsibility, and made them, once again, members of the moral community. Much of what Big Nurse says to and about the men is couched in these terms. The men, she suggests, are like children; they need to grow up and act like adults. Moreover, the explicit explanation of the group confession sessions is that the men learn to get along in the group so that they will be able to get along in society. The men in the therapeutic community are to learn how to "measure up" so they will not be labelled insane: "Bring these old sins into the open where they can be washed by the sight of all."[1]

A second rationale for the asylum was that "relearning one's place" was important in rehabilitation of the insane. The asylum was seen as a refuge from a world full of temptations. The horror of attempting to rise above one's station was a theme characteristic of the early years of the asylum in America. Even in the America of the early 1960s, when Kesey was writing his novel, and when the ethic of upward mobility was strong and pervasive, one heard resonances of this earlier idea. For example, much of Big Nurse's attempts at control are couched in terms of "knowing one's place" in the world of the asylum, of being obedient, deferential, and nondisruptive. Indeed, as Chief Bromden muses, the function of the asylum is to get people "adjusted" or "fixed" (p. 40) so that they can assume their proper role in the scheme of things. Part of McMurphy's threat to Big Nurse is his threat to an ideology which seeks to pin people down in narrow, rigidly defined roles and positions. McMurphy is a wanderer, a loner, an opportunist. One can imagine that superintendents in the early asylums would have perceived McMurphy as the perfect example of the problems for which the asylum was created. Today, of course, he is called "psychopathic."

A third rationale for the asylum was that it would serve to protect society from the insane. Fear of the insane in society is reflected most strongly in Kesey's novel during the expedition to the sea. The patients, McMurphy, and Dr. Spivey stop in a gas station on the way to the boat dock. The garage attendant, at first reluctant to give service and scornful of this unkempt group of human beings, is frightened into action by McMurphy's revelation about the men's identity and their proclivity for uncontrolled violence. This scene dramatizes clearly a pervasive social fear of the insane person, a fear that he is capable of uncontrolled and unpredictable aggression. We are socialized in this society to inhibit the spontaneous expression of aggression. This inhibition no doubt reflects the degree to which social action is rationalized and made predictable. It has been suggested that the insane, the "mentally ill," serve as fantasy objects, that is, as vehicles which stimulate our own desires to express aggression and other strong impulses. However that may be, there is no doubt that spontaneous, unpredictable impulse-expression is associated with the popular stereotype of mental illness in our society.

All three of these rationales for incarceration of the insane are aspects of social control. Any society needs to be able to handle those events or persons that threaten to disrupt what it defines as the orderly working of its processes. These controls are most effective, of course, when they are socialized or "built in," preferably at an early age. All societies have some idea of matching persons with positions, and enforce this to some extent, and all societies make some provision for dealing with transgressors by singling them out for punishment. It is perhaps uncomfortable to think of the mentally ill as deviants in the same way that ordinary criminals are deviants. Yet both of these groups do, in a sense, serve as examples to the rest of us, particularly of the fate which can be ours if we fall from grace. It is not for nothing, then, that Kesey's asylum stands, with its tall and massive walls and barred windows, lonely and isolated in the distant fields of rural Oregon.

In portraying the asylum as such an unpleasant kind of place, and one in which almost no curing of insanity is possible, Kesey may have contributed to the growing trend away from viewing insanity as a disease best treated by incarceration. We should be careful about attributing too much influence to this novel, for the trend had begun before Kesey's novel was published. Nevertheless, when the history of the treatment of insanity is written with more perspective than we now have, it may well appear that Kesey's novel, by exaggerating the inadequacy of the asylum in dealing with the problems of the insane, has made a small but important contribution to the history of mental care in America.

Notes

1. Ken Kesey, *One Flew Over the Cuckoo's Nest* (New York: New American Library, 1962), p. 48. All subsequent references are to this edition, and are parenthesized within the text.

2. I am indebted especially to the following works for many of the historical trends dealt with in this paper: Michael Foucault, *Madness and Civilization* (New York: Random House, 1965); Robert Perruci, *Circle of Madness: On Being Insane and Institutionalized in America* (Englewood Cliffs, N.J.: Prentice-Hall, 1974); George Rosen, *Madness in Society* (New York: Harper and Row, 1968); David Rothman, *The Discovery of the Asylum: Social Order and Disorder in the New Republic* (New York: Little, Brown, 1971); Thomas Scheff, *Being Mentally Ill* (Chicago: Aldine, 1966).

5

Big Mama, Big Papa, and Little Sons in Ken Kesey's *One Flew Over the Cuckoo's Nest*

■■■■■■■■■■■■■■■

Ruth Sullivan

Sigmund Freud is something less than a culture hero in Ken Kesey's *One Flew Over the Cuckoo's Nest*. What else but destructive can one call a psychoanalytically informed therapy that brands McMurphy's rebellion against the institution's ego-murder as "schizophrenic reaction," his love of "poozle" and pretty girls as "Latent Homosexual with Reaction Formation" or, with emphasis, "Negative Oedipal"?[1] Kesey portrays the psychiatrists and residents as patsies of Big Nurse Ratched, and portrays her as a power-maniac running a small machine within that big machine, Society (the "Combine"). Psychoanalytic therapy in this novel dehumanizes because it serves not people but technology.

Ironic then, is the fact that while the novel disparages psychoanalytic therapy, it compliments psychoanalytic theory in that Kesey

Originally published in *Literature and Psychology* 25: 1 (1975), pp. 34–44. Reprinted by permission.

structures human relationships in *Cuckoo's Nest* after his own understanding of Freud's delineation of the Oedipus complex.[2] That is, Kesey presents the typical oedipal triangle of mother, father, and sons in Nurse Ratched, Randle McMurphy, and Chief Bromden plus the other inmates of the asylum. And he dramatizes some typical oedipal conflicts: the sons witness encounters, often explicitly sexual, between the father and mother figures, and the crucial emotional issue for the sons is how to define their manliness in relation to the mother figure and with the help of and ability to identify with the father.

That Kesey intends Nurse Ratched to play Big Mama not only to Chief Bromden but also to the other characters is evident by the many references to her often perverted maternal qualities. To Public Relations she is "just like a mother" (p. 37). He believes in "that tender little mother crap" (p. 57) as McMurphy puts it, but the big Irishman and soon the other inmates see through "that smiling flour-faced old mother" (p. 48) with her "big, womanly breasts" (p. 11). Chief Bromden observes Big Nurse draw Billy's "cheek to her starched breast, stroking his shoulder. . . ." Meanwhile, "she continued to glare at us as she spoke. It was strange to hear that voice, soft and soothing and warm as a pillow, coming out of a face hard as porcelain" (p. 265). "We are victims of a matriarchy here, my friend" (p. 59), Harding says to McMurphy. "Man has but *one* truly effective weapon against that juggernaut of modern matriarchy" (p. 66), rape, and McMurphy is elected to do it.

Why rape? Because Kesey's Big Mama is a "ball-cutter" (p. 57), in McMurphy's language, and the men must protect themselves. Harding, too, understands that one of Big Nurse's most effective methods of control is to render the men impotent: Dr. Spivey by subtle insinuations about his need for drugs and by depriving him of real authority; Billy Bibbit, by threatening to tell his mother about his night with the prostitute; and the young residents by making them fear her judgment on their professional performance. "There's not a man here that isn't afraid he is losing or has already lost his whambam," says Harding. "We comical little creatures can't even achieve masculinity in the rabbit world, that's how weak and inadequate we are. Hee. We are the *rabbits*, one might say, of the rabbit world!" (p. 63) Harding even sees that to the Nurse, lobotomies are symbolic castrations: "Yes; chopping away the brain. Frontal-lobe castration. I guess if she can't cut below the belt she'll do it above the eyes" (p. 165).

Big Nurse should be keeping those in her care warm and fed and healthy; she should be loving but is instead denying, destructive, and terrifying. Big Daddy, in Randle McMurphy's Big Daddyhood, is only a little less obvious than Nurse Ratched's warped maternity. "Like the logger, . . . the swaggering gambler . . . the cowboy out of the TV set . . ." (p. 172), Randle McMurphy booms upon the scene, his heels striking fire out of the tiles, his huge seamed hand extended to lift the inmates out of fear and into freedom. He renews their almost lost sense of manliness by denying Harding's description of them as "rabbits *sans* whambam" (p. 63), by having them deep-sea fish, gamble, and party it up with pretty little whores, by encouraging the men (himself as an example) to flirt with the nurses, by spinning virility fantasies, and by introducing Billy to women. He teaches them to laugh and to revolt against Ratched's tyranny, and he often protects them while they are growing.

McMurphy plays father to all the inmates, but Chief Bromden makes explicit the Irishman's fatherly role by often comparing him to the Chief's own father. "He talks a little the way Papa used to. . . . He's as broad as Papa was tall . . . and he's hard in a different kind of way from Papa" (p. 16). "He's finally getting cagey, is all. The way Papa finally did . . ." (p. 150). Chief Bromden learns from and is protected by McMurphy even as the small Indian boy learned to hunt from a father who tried to save the Columbia Indian's heritage for his tribe and son. "McMurphy was teaching me. I was feeling better than I'd remembered feeling since I was a kid . . ." (p. 216). Chief Bromden grows big: he lifts and destroys the control panel; he frees himself from Big Nurse, the Combine, and his insanity; and he performs an act of love and mercy by killing the husk of the once mighty McMurphy and by assuming the manhood McMurphy bestowed upon him. The big Irishman seems to pump life and blood into the Indian:

> *I remember the fingers were thick and strong closing over*
> *mine, and my hand commenced to feel peculiar and went*
> *to swelling up there on my stick of an arm, like he was*
> *transmitting his own blood into it. It rang with blood*
> *and power. It blowed up near as big as his, I*
> *remember. . . . (p. 27)*

In fact, McMurphy encourages the Chief to surpass his model. Christ-like, the father sacrifices himself so that his sons may live as free men.

Kesey sketches in the oedipal triangle, then, in dramatizing an intense emotional relationship among father, mother, and son figures and by having the father teach the sons what it means to be a man. He teaches them about self-assertion, aggression, fun, and sex—the latter sometimes in relationship to Big Nurse. After all, the inmates expect McMurphy to make Ratched into a woman by performing some sexual act with her and McMurphy eventually does that. Meanwhile, he acts sexually toward her by making teasing remarks about her big breasts.

But Kesey gives the reader his own unique version of the oedipal struggle. What the sons witness in the interaction between Big Nurse and Randle McMurphy is pseudosex. The most urgent emotional isue between them is really power. McMurphy will strip Big Nurse, but he will do so in vengeful destruction of her power. When he teases her about her womanly body suppressed by the starched uniform, his motive is to humiliate her. When he takes up the inmates' challenge to best Big Nurse he says:

> *I've never seen a woman I thought was more than me, I don't care whether I can get it up for her or not. . . . So I'm saying five bucks to each of you that wants it I can't put a betsy bug up that nurse's butt within a week. . . . Just that. A bee in her butt, a burr in her bloomers. Get her goat. (pp. 68–69)*

The imagery here is not genital but anal. He wants to be free of her control, wants to be in control himself, and wants the inmates to gain self-control and control over Big Nurse. So, the central symbolic act in the novel and the unseating and destruction of the control panel. Big Nurse herself is a caricature of the anal personality, a typical obsessive-compulsive creature with those typical needs for order, cleanliness, and power, with the tendency to treat people like objects, the inability to relax and to relate to others with tolerance for their frailties. Chief Bromden associates her with machinery, whiteness, frost, starch, cleanliness, rules, time, manipulation, and the Combine. She does try to castrate her sons, but it is in the interest of power. She denies them warmth, autonomy, and manhood in order to keep her own world intact. Her biggest fear, and the sign of her defeat, is loss of control.

It seems, then, that in Kesey's version of the oedipal struggle, the sons learn that mature women are dangerous because they want to emasculate (i.e, to control so as to incapacitate) their men. Almost every woman who stands in an explicitly sexual relationship to men in the novel poses a threat to her man's virility. Billy Bibbit's mother and the wives of Harding and Ruckly ("Fffffffuck da wife!" [p. 27]) are the most blatant examples. Harding's wife, for instance, makes cutting comments about his effeminate mannerisms and flitty friends during a visit to the asylum in which she wears blood-red nail polish on sharp fingernails, high heels that make her as tall as her husband, and a blouse so low-cut that when she provocatively bends over, Chief Bromden can see down it from across the room. "I am a woman," she says in effect, "but I am more of a man than you are."

Even for McMurphy, set forth as an almost legendary lover, women are often aggressive bitches without tenderness or generosity. When McMurphy recalls the occasion on which he lost his virginity he seems not delighted but sad. That nine-year-old "little whore" (p. 217) callously presented her ten-year-old lover with her dress as a memento of an act that McMurphy had wished to sanctify. She was the "first girl ever drug me to bed" (p. 217) he says, and "from that day to this it seemed I might as well live up to my name—dedicated lover . . ." (p. 218). McMurphy does not embrace the role as eagerly as his boasts on other occasions seem to indicate, for in telling his tale, his expression is "woebegone" and in the dark, when he thinks no one can see him, his face "is dreadfully tired and strained and *frantic*" (p. 218). The event seems disillusioning partly because, boylike, he believed that sex and commitment were complements (he proposed to the girl) but discovered that for his girl they were not—partly, perhaps, because she, rather than he, was the aggressor. McMurphy jokes about this—about the underaged and oversexed girl who got him arrested for statutory rape, for instance—but the pattern in the novel seems nevertheless constant: aggressive women hurt their men.

The women in Chief Bromden's past were almost always ball-cutting bitches, too, beginning with that female responsible for cheating the Columbian Indians of their land. She was "an old white-haired woman in an outfit so stiff and heavy it must be armor plate" (p. 179). She plotted to have the offer to buy made "by mistake" to Mrs. Bromden, for she knew instinctively that women, and not men, wore the trousers there. She was right. Mrs. Bromden made Chief Tee Ah Millatoona little: "Oh, the Combine's big—big. He fought it a long time till my mother made him too little to fight any more and he gave up" (p. 187). By overmanagement, Mrs. Bromden ruined her husband and her son, too. So the sons in *Cuckoo's Nest* learn that the only women who are fun and harmless are not mature women but girls, sisterly girls who are easily controlled and undemanding. The feminine ideals in this novel are Candy and Sandy because they bring joy and warmth into the asylum. But they do not need to be taken seriously: they are whores, they can scarcely be distinguished from one another, and they are like children. Kesey makes them sentimental portraits, whores-with-hearts-of-gold whose younger-sister role is made explicit by Chief Bromden when he describes McMurphy and one of the "girls" at the end of the night: "I could see McMurphy and the girl snuggled into each other's shoulders, getting comfortable, more like two tired little kids than a grown man and a grown woman in bed together to make love" (pp. 258–59). In fact, Candy and Sandy are most closely associated with the childish fun of the party, where the liquor is as much sticky-sweet cough syrup as vodka, and the principal delight lies in fooling the grown-ups—Big Nurse and her night supervisors—who think that the children are asleep when really they are playing through the night. Even Billy's sexual initiation by Candy is more infantile than adult. The scene in which Big Nurse intrudes upon Billy's love nest is rather like a parent's discovery of children engaged in forbidden games (Ratched threatens to tell Billy's mother)—a discovery followed by the child's response of extreme guilt. Billy first denies all responsibility and tattles on his friends; then he commits suicide as self-punishment.

Kesey's oedipal triangle, then, is not casebook pure. It bears the stamp of the preceding emotional phase, the anal, in which the crucial issues are control over one's own body and the environment, rebellion and submission, autonomy and shame. Such a pattern works itself out in the novel thus: the oedipal elements revolve around the wish of the sons to love and be loved by adult women and by the women originally closest to them, mother and Big Nurse. They turn to the father, McMurphy, as role model; he teaches them by anecdote and example how to be men. The anal elements color this pattern because the sons are frustrated in their desires toward a woman as threatening as Big Nurse. They want to be men, but she wants them to be automatons; they want to love, but she wants to control. Because Big Nurse manages every aspect of their lives—their bodies, activities, shelter—she deprives them of autonomy. Oedipal elements mixed with anal reappear when McMurphy both "feminizes" Big Nurse, in his symbolic rape that exposes her breasts, and dethrones her, breaks her control.

Further, the novel displays emotional conflicts even more primitive than these, for if the men fear woman because she can emasculate her man (a phallic issue) or because she can control him (an anal issue), they also fear her because she withholds emotional warmth and physical care (oral issues). A deep disappointment that the novel expresses concerning women is not only their failure to be equal and generous partners to men, or even their unwillingness to submit to men in a battle of the sexes, but their failure to play a warmly maternal role, or, when actually assuming that role, their failure to play it effectively.

Though Nurse Ratched is an obvious example of this, almost all other women in the novel are, too. The birthmarked nurse, for example, cannot take adequate care of the men because she fears and hates them, holds them responsible for her "dirtiness," as she conceives of her birthmark.

> In the morning she sees how she's stained again and
> somehow she figures it's not really from inside her—how
> could it be? a good Catholic girl like her?—and she
> figures it's on account of working evenings among a
> whole wardful of people like me [Chief Bromden]. It's all
> our fault, and she's going to get us for it if it's the last
> thing she does. (pp. 143–44)

Even the Japanese nurse, who has more sensitivity than any other woman in that institution, who understands why everyone hates Ratched, and who wants to help McMurphy and Chief Bromden after their fight with Washington—even she is ineffectual. Chief Bromden describes her as "about as big as the small end of nothing whittled to a fine point. . . ." She has "little bird bones in her face" and her hands are little, "full of pink birthday candles" (p. 233). She is maternal but not powerful enough to ensure her men's safety.

One motherly person appreciatively portrayed in the novel is Chief

Bromden's grandmother, who, "dust in her wrinkles," sat beside the small boy at the salmon falls and counted on his fingers "Tingle, tingle, tremble toes, she's a good fisherman, catches hens, puts 'em inna pens . . . wire blier, limber lock, three geese inna flock . . . one flew east, one flew west, one flew over the cuckoo's nest . . ." (p. 239). The Chief says, "I like the game and I like Grandma" (p. 239), for she is a loving woman associated with all that is healthy in the Chief's background—his Indian heritage, the natural order, and the warm bond his people felt for one another. But like the Japanese nurse who cannot for long protect her men, this old woman could not save her men from moral and mental disintegration. Her son, the Chief, becomes a drunken derelict and her grandson falls insane. "Next time I saw her she was stone cold dead . . ." (p. 239). In effect, she abandons them when they are most needy and the nursery rhyme she chants is in certain ways a sinister prefiguration of what will happen to the Chief and his son. The rhyme is about *a woman* who catches things and puts them in pens (like Big Nurse, who pens up "Chief Broom") and about a dispersing flock of geese (like, perhaps, the dispersal of the Columbia Indian tribe and of their salmon), one of whom flies over the cuckoo's nest, over the mental institution that for the Chief is both an escape from the world (a nest) and a prison. So the loving grandmother is shown abandoning her sons and indirectly predicting their defeat. Women who should be able to help and protect, or at least take care of, their men are often disappointing in *Cuckoo's Nest*.

Then there is Harding's wife, who more than castrates him and beats him in a power struggle. She also actually denies him the emotional support and tenderness he needs, a failure symbolized (as with Nurse Ratched) by her outsized breasts: "one hell of a set of cha-bobs. . . . Big as Old Lady Ratched's" (p. 159), McMurphy says. Now, Mrs. Harding's breasts signal for Harding her especially active sexuality and sexual appeal, but unconsciously such breasts likely stir remembrances of motherly giving, a quality in which Mrs. Harding is deficient.

So is Nurse Ratched—the most formidable woman in the novel and possessor of the most formidable bosom. All the men are impressed, but Chief Bromden seems to express for all of them the deep yearning that Big Nurse's actions should answer the promise of her anatomy—the promise of softness and abundant giving one can associate with a mother's breasts. Instead, she seems to the Chief to resent her body and to work hard to suppress it in her starched, clean white uniform. He is deeply troubled by this as by the porcelain-and-plastic quality of her face, the burning cold or burning heat of her lipstick and nail polish, in fact by many aspects of her body. He fixes upon it almost obsessively and upon her emotional states, to which he is attuned as closely as an anxious child is attuned to his mother. His fixation upon her body is discriminating, though. He is captured by the quality of the whole body in its stiff uniform, then by her breasts, face, mouth, eyes, and hands; not the hips, say, or the belly or shoulders, but all those portions of anatomy on which a child focuses in relating to his mother. And when he observes these body parts, it is with anxious eagerness to know her mood (it is almost always dangerous).

> Her painted smile twists, stretches to an open snarl
> (p. 11).

> Gradually the lips gather together again under the little
> white nose, run together, like the red-hot wire had got hot
> enough to melt, shimmer a second, then click solid as the
> molten metal sets, growing cold and strangely dull. Her
> lips part, and her tongue comes between them a chunk of
> slag. Her eyes open again, and they have that strange
> dull and cold and flat look the lips have . . . (p. 90).

> She darted the eyes out with every word, stabbing at the
> men's faces . . . (p. 262).

> Her more than ever white hand skittered on the pad like
> one of those arcade gypsies that scratch out fortunes for a
> penny (p. 168).

Chief Bromden's dramatized need for a warm mother is appropriate to his condition as schizophrenic; his emotional regression is often so severe that he withdraws from reality completely (retreats into the fog), refuses to speak or acknowledge that he can hear, and cannot control body functions. The emotional pattern Kesey draws for Chief Bromden is severe withdrawal alternating with periods of intense, if often negative, fixation on a mother figure, then apparent growth to attachment to a father, and finally growth beyond an infantile need for a family.

It is impossible to know accurately how much of Kesey's delineation of the Oedipus complex is deliberate and how much is inevitable revelation of his own complexes. He clearly labels his Big Mama, Big Daddy, and little sons; but when he involves them in a power struggle and in a search for a generous, caretaking mother, likely his emotional constellations are no longer consciously created. But our subject is not biography; it is interpretation of one work of art. Hence we might ask how Kesey's oral, anal, and oedipal patterns, deliberate and not, influence a reader's emotional response and interpretation of themes.

For instance, one might wonder what psychological events make the novel so especially appealing to the young (and others). Big Mama is indeed defeated, and Chief Bromden does escape as do several other inmates, but the victory is pyrrhic. Cheswick, Billy Bibbit, and most crucially, Randle McMurphy are all sacrificed to achieve that end. Furthermore, the novel promises that there will be more Big Nurses in the future.

> *They talk for a while about whether she's the root of all
> the trouble here or not, and Harding says she's the root
> of most of it. Most of the other guys think so too, but
> McMurphy isn't so sure any more. He says he thought
> so at one time but now he don't know. He says he don't
> think getting her out of the way would really make much
> difference; he says there's something bigger making all
> this mess and goes on to try to say what he thinks it is.
> (p. 165)*

Chief Bromden knows what it is:

> *McMurphy doesn't know it, but he's onto what I realized
> a long time back, that it's not just the Big Nurse by
> herself, but it's the whole Combine, the nation-wide
> Combine that's the really big force, and the nurse is just
> a high-ranking official for them. (p. 165)*

In oedipal terms, the novel promises that the matriarchy cannot be defeated. To do battle with it means the castration of the father and most of the sons—indeed, all of the sons, for the rehabilitation of Chief Bromden is fairy tale, not reality. He has been on the ward nearly twenty years; he has had over two hundred shock treatments; and he is, by the revelations of his own speech, a paranoid schizophrenic. A man so deeply scarred is unlikely to recover so completely in a few months, no matter how brilliant his model and nurturer is.

This anxiety-filled fantasy of mechanical, destructive motherhood cannot account for the enthusiasm of Kesey's readers any more than can the genius of the style or plotting. The latter two are significant, of course, but for reasons beyond the aesthetic or intellectual pleasures they afford. The novel must also create other, more satisfying fantasies, as well as a defense against its nuclear fantasy that is effective enough to make a reader, especially a young one, feel not only reassured but triumphant.

One of the appeals of the novel is the opportunity it affords its readers to feel unjustly persecuted and to revel in self-pity: "Poor little me. See how helpless and good I am; yet They hurt me." Because persecution of those undeserving sets the tone for *One Flew Over the Cuckoo's Nest*, a reader can scarcely escape the novel's stimulation of these unconscious feelings in himself. Everyone has in his early life experienced the apparent omnipotence and omniscience of adults who, on occasion, must frustrate the demands of their infants and must therefore seem unjust, even cruel. But such experiences are usually painful. Why should their arousal in *Cuckoo's Nest* prove delightful? Because, first, the novel is convincing about the power of the Combine and its agent, Nurse Ratched. Americans particularly have reason to feel oppressed by Big Government, Big Business, and Big Industry and to be convinced that the individual alone can do little to influence them to his benefit or to prevent their harming him. Chief Bromden is paranoic, but not everything in his vision is false: "You think the guy telling this is ranting and raving my *God;* you think this is too horrible to have really happened, this is too awful to be the truth! . . . But it's the truth even if it didn't happen" (p. 13). The novel offers its readers a sympathetic forum, a justification for feeling oppressed, even congratulations for being so sensitive as to have those feelings. Kesey's novel says, in effect, that someone understands.

A second reason for the pleasure-in-persecution feelings evoked in the reader's unconscious by *Cuckoo's Nest* is this: "poor little me" fantasies are pleasurable if one knows that one's audience is kindly and even effective against the alleged or actual abuse. The antiestablishment, antityranny tone of the novel answers these needs: so does the person of McMurphy because he functions the way a powerful father figure might against a cruel mother. The plaint of injustice is largely carried by the helpless inmates; their target is Big Nurse and the Combine; their forum and protection is McMurphy. Finally, one might speculate that being unjustly persecuted is pleasant if it arouses one's masochism and if it provides a sense of moral superiority: "You may be bigger than I am but I am superior to you in other, especially moral, ways." *Cuckoo's Nest* dramatically demonstrates the righteousness and goodness of the inmates over Big Nurse, her cohorts, and the Combine. And of course she is overthrown. Injustice may live, but in *Cuckoo's Nest* it does not thrive.

The novel also richly gratifies latent or conscious hostile impulses against authority. Obviously, the novel delights in jibes and pain inflicted upon Nurse Ratched. (An audience applaudes whenever Big Nurse is bested in the play; it even hisses and boos when the actress who plays her takes her bow.) But the book allows expression of hostile impulses toward loved authorities as well, for the inmates not only care about McMurphy, they also resent him. Big Nurse succeeds in turning most of them against him for a while when she hints that he exploits them. Billy Bibbit turns against him when caught in his sexual misdemeanor. They all use him to fight their battles, egg him on to engage Big Nurse when they, but not McMurphy, know that he can be punished in the "Brain Murdering" room. Most significantly, they kill him. They are responsible for his lobotomy: "We couldn't stop him [from attacking Big Nurse] because we were the ones making him do it. It wasn't the Nurse that was forcing him, it was our need that was making him push himself slowly up . . ." (p. 267).

Chief Bromden performs an actual killing. Manifestly, the deed is euthanasia; symbolically, it is an enacted crucifixion; thematically, it is evidence that the son has grown up and surpassed his father even while loving him; and latently, the killing expresses the ancient hostility of the son to even a loving father.

To permission for indulgence in self-pity and attacks on loved and hated authority figures, the novel adds permission to gratify dependency wishes. A dominant theme of *One Flew Over the Cuckoo's Nest* concerns the nature of individual freedom—political, social, and psychological. It asserts that in the psychological realm, certain kinds of dependence are healthy: the dependence of a child upon good parents, of a patient upon effective nurses and doctors, and of weak adults upon nurturing strong ones. But this dependent condition is healthy only if it fosters eventual independence. Big Nurse destroys because she must control; hence she blocks the autonomy of her patients, whereas McMurphy nurtures because, while he protects, he also encourages the inmates to use their own resources in order to meet the world. This theme, readily apparent to a reader's intelligence, disguises the abundant latent gratification the novel offers one's often unacknowledged pleasure in dependency upon an omnipotent figure. Throughout the novel, with a few exceptions, McMurphy acts on behalf of the patients, acts so magnificently that a reader laughs. "We ain't ordinary nuts; we're every bloody one of us hot off the criminal-insane ward, on our way to San Quentin where they got better facilities to handle us" (p. 199–200); so McMurphy informs the gas station attendants who would bully the inmates. Here the weak overpower the strong the way children overpower giants in fairy tales. The inmates overpower Big Nurse when McMurphy, a sort of kindly helper figure also common in fairy tales, shows them how; and they overpower her, in part gayly and jokingly, in part grimly. The childlike fun of the novel, the use of ridicule as a weapon against oppression, and the demonstration on the part of McMurphy that he is a bigger, better person than Big Bad Nurse all contribute to a reader's readiness to accept the novel's tacit invitation: allow yourself to depend upon the good, omnipotent father; he will help you conquer the wicked stepmother.

Cuckoo's Nest is gratifying especially to the young, then, because while it creates an anxiety-ridden fantasy about a destructive mother (and social order), it also creates a powerful, caring father to allay anxiety. In addition, it grants indulgence in certain unconscious needs and wishes to be dependent, to feel unjustly treated (masochistic and moral-righteousness pleasures), and to attack and defeat ambivalently held authority figures (even McMurphy is killed).

To unearth unconscious fantasies as a way of understanding why *One Flew Over the Cuckoo's Nest* is emotionally satisfying is not to dismiss the power or validity of themes one understands intellectually. Indeed, unconscious fantasies isolated from theme in a piece of fiction sound grotesque, perhaps meaningless. In *Cuckoo's Nest*, as in all fiction, theme not only gives meaning to unconscious fantasy but also functions as a kind of defense.[3] For instance, *Cuckoo's Nest* is usually read as an indictment of our technological society, which, by standardization and forced conformity, murders human brains, even as the shock shop murders the inmates' minds. Psychotherapy is dangerous, this novel alleges, because it has become mechanized, a tool for social control wielded by the Combine. But the novel also affirms that man's drive for independence is so strong that no matter how overwhelming the obstacles, he will break free; it suggests, as well, that perhaps nature will once more nurture man where technology now destroys him.

Kesey's antitechnology, pronature theme is fittingly supported by his deliberate use of an oedipal triangle marked by a man-woman power struggle, a triangle in which mother acts like a machine against, rather than for, her children, while father tries valiantly to restore them to their own natures and to freedom. The unconscious needs the novel stimulates in its readers also re-enforce the theme. For instance, though men yearn to be free, they also fear autonomy and wish to be dependent. Chief Bromden sits in the cuckoo's nest because he has not the courage to face the world. No more do those voluntarily committed—Billy Bibbit and Harding, say, who admit their fear of leaving the institution.

Now *Cuckoo's Nest* has another theme that seems to counterpoint its blatant Darwinian survival-of-the-fittest message. The strong do indeed aggress against the weak; and though a few escape the trap, most are caught and destroyed. But the Combine is only the ostensible enemy; the real one lurks in men's own minds. Just as in a paranoid fantasy the external persecutors are projections of the sufferer's self-hatred, so is the Combine a projection of the destructive power-drive in men—especially in weak, ineffectual men. While *Cuckoo's Nest* does show how the strong oppress the weak, it also shows how the weak can destroy the strong. Chief Bromden understands this at the end of the novel, for he knows that McMurphy attacks Nurse Ratched because the inmates compel him to. Harding understood this earlier. In explaining why he must be institutionalized, he at first blames society:

> It wasn't the practices, I don't think, it was the feeling
> that the great, deadly, pointing forefinger of society was
> pointing at me—and the great voice of millions chanting,
> "Shame. Shame. Shame." It's society's way of dealing
> with someone different. (p. 257)

But McMurphy counters that he, too, is different, yet he was not seriously affected. Harding answers:

> *"I wasn't giving my reason as the sole reason. Though I used to think at one time, a few years ago . . . that society's chastising was the sole force that drove one along the road to crazy [sic] . . . you've caused me to re-appraise my theory. There's something else that drives people, strong people like you, my friend, down that road. . . . It is us!"* Harding swept his hand about him *in a soft white circle and repeated, "Us." (pp. 257–58)*

The theme of *Cuckoo's Nest* is not merely the assertion that society will get you. It also realistically affirms that if society gets you, it is because you have complied in both your own and others' destruction. The weak are tyrants, too, subtle and dangerous because they can wake in the strong a sympathetic identification and perhaps guilt: "Why should I have so much when they have so little? Then, maybe I am in some way responsible for their fate." Like the inmates of the asylum, the weak can unintentionally exploit and cannibalize their benefactors, driving them to ruin.

This more subtle theme functions as defense in the novel, because without it *Cuckoo's Nest* would offer a sentimental, oversimple diagnosis of an individual's ills, rather than dramatizing without moralizing a complex relationship between man and his society. The novel is idealistic, but not at the expense of clearsightedness. It abundantly gratifies the id, but it also recognizes the needs of an ego that must bring the psyche into harmony with the real world and the demands of a superego that will not condone flagrant abuses of morality: the guilty are punished. Witness the fate of Nurse Ratched—and of Randle McMurphy for mauling her.[4]

Unlike, say, Tolstoi's *Kreutzer Sonata*, whose condemnation of social conventions is transparently paranoic, hence clearly not to be taken as seriously as the protagonist's psychology, *Cuckoo's Nest* almost from the beginning tempers its antitechnology theme with realism. Everywhere in the novel the ego has control over a potentially too-rapacious superego and a demanding id. For instance, Chief Bromden is the narrator; he is a paranoid schizophrenic, hence the world he describes is his world, not everyone's. Then, as the Chief comes more and more often out of the fog, his perceptions grow more accurate. For a long time he sees McMurphy as "a giant come out of the sky to save us from the Combine that was networking the land with copper wire and crystal" (p. 224); later he understands the man's weaknesses—that is, his humanity. He at first believed that McMurphy might save them; he later sees that the men are using him and that they must eventually save themselves. Finally, while the novel does permit Chief Bromden to fly like a goose northward home, it tempers the promise that Chief Bromden's freedom is hazard-free. For Kesey implicitly compares the Chief's escape scene with another in which the latter sees clearly for the first time where he is, in an asylum deep in the country. A lively, revelling dog investigates the countryside while "the moon glistened around him in the wet grass . . ." (p. 143). Then the Chief listens attentively to Canada honkers flying above, "a black, weaving necklace, drawn into a V by that lead goose . . . a black cross opening and closing . . ." (p. 143). Finally, he runs off

> *in the direction they [the geese] had gone, toward the*
> *highway. . . . Then I could hear a car speed up out of a*
> *turn. The headlights loomed over the rise and peered*
> *ahead down the highway. I watched the dog and the car*
> *making for the same spot of pavement. (p. 143)*

The Chief has identified with the geese, flying free after a lead goose, even as he and the others do when led by that "Bull Goose Loony" McMurphy, later to crucify himself ("Do I get a crown of thorns?" [p. 237]) for them. He identifies with the dog, too, young and free and curious about his environment but also heading for potential death on the highway. Once more, natural things are threatened by machines. Will the Chief, too, be crushed?

> *I ran across the grounds in the direction I remembered*
> *seeing the dog go, toward the highway. . . . I caught a*
> *ride with a guy, a Mexican guy, going north in a truck*
> *full of sheep. . . . (p. 272)*

Kesey does not mislead his readers. For those who choose to hear, he says that while the social order is indeed a mighty, complex organism difficult to understand and more difficult to influence or change, nevertheless men are responsible for their own fates. One must be strong to survive, even stronger to prevail, but if such a man is inspirited with that most valued of American qualities—the drive for independence and freedom—he can make it.

Kesey's novel is a kind of phenomenon, though, for the skillful way in which he manages to be hard-headedly realistic (hence to appeal to the ego), as well as indulgent of so many and such powerful unconscious, even infantile drives (the novel richly gratifies the id) and respectful of certain ethical considerations: the evil are punished, but so are those who inflict punishment; crime does not pay (the superego is appeased). The fact that the theme can be doubly perceived—technology is responsible for man's destruction and men are responsible for their own—both stimulates and manages the anxiety-ridden nuclear fantasy. On the one hand, a reader can fully respond to his own regressive fantasies, and on the other, he is encouraged to pull out of them and cope with external reality. Kesey's use of the oedipal constellation to pattern human relationships in *Cuckoo's Nest* functions in much the same way. The content of the novel damns psychoanalytically informed psychotherapy in such a way as to cater to fantasies of persecution and helplessness; meanwhile, the novel's artistic design uses psychoanalytic theory to reassure the reader (as all skillful handling of artistic form and style does) that nevertheless everything is safe. It is as though Kesey says: "I, the artist, can handle this material, dangerous though it may be. See, I make it part of the solid structure of this novel. You need not be afraid while I am in control." Mama may be dangerous, but Big Daddy is here to protect his children.

Notes

1. Ken Kesey, *One Flew Over the Cuckoo's Nest* (New York: Signet, 1962), p. 135. Henceforth, all quotations from the novel will come from this edition. Page numbers will be noted in my text.

2. Ken Kesey worked in a mental institution while writing *Cuckoo's Nest* and he knew of Freudian psychology through Vic Lovell, to whom the novel is dedicated ("To Vik [sic] Lovell, who told me dragons did not exist, then led me to their lairs") who Tom Wolfe says was "like a young Viennese analyst, or at least a California graduate school version of one. . . . He introduced Kesey to Freudian psychology. Kesey had never run into a system of thought like this before." (Tom Wolfe, *The Electric Kool-Aid Acid Test* [New York: Bantam, 1969], p. 36.)

3. For this theory and for most of the psychoanalytic literary methodology in my essay, I am indebted to Norman N. Holland's works, especially to *The Dynamics of Literary Response* (New York: Oxford University Press, 1968).

4. For further elucidation of how fiction satisfies all parts of the psyche, see Simon O. Lesser, *Fiction and the Unconscious* (Boston: Beacon Press, 1957), passim.

6

The Grail Knight Arrives: Ken Kesey, *One Flew Over the Cuckoo's Nest*

◆◆◆◆◆◆◆◆◆◆◆◆◆◆◆

Raymond M. Olderman

Randle Patrick McMurphy sweeps into the asylum wasteland of Ken Kesey's *One Flew Over the Cuckoo's Nest* like April coming to T. S. Eliot's wasteland: "mixing / Memory and desire, stirring / Dull roots with spring rain." He literally drags the unwilling asylum wastelanders out of the tranquilized fog that protects them—a fog that is forever "snowing down cold and white all over,"[1] where they try to hide "in forgetful snow, feeding / A little life with dried tubers." And, by dragging them from their retreat, he cures the Fisher King, Chief Bromden—a six-foot-eight-inch giant from a tribe of "fish Injuns," who is wounded, like all other wastelanders, in his manhood. The cure takes hold most dramatically on a fishing trip when McMurphy supplies the Chief and eleven other disciples with drink for their thirst, a woman for their desires, stimulation for their memories, and some badly needed self-respect for their shriveled souls—and all this despite the fact that the Chief "fears death by water." ("Afraid I'd step in over my head and drown, be sucked off down the drain and clean

Originally published in *Beyond the Waste Land: The American Novel in the Nineteen-Sixties* (Yale University Press, 1972), pp. 35–51. Reprinted by permission. Copyright 1972, Yale University, New Haven, CT 06520.

out to sea. I used to be real brave around water when I was a kid"
[p. 169].) The silent Chief's voice is restored and he becomes the
prophet who narrates the tale, while the false prophet—the enemy,
the Big Nurse, Madam Sosostris, who has the "movement of a tarot-
card reader in a glass arcade case" (p. 188)—is deprived of her voice
in the last moments of the book.

The tale takes place in the ward of an insane asylum where an
iron-minded, frost-hearted nurse rules by means of one twentieth-
century version of brutality—mental and spiritual debilitation. Her
patients are hopeless "Chronics" and "Vegetables," or they are "Acutes"
who do not, according to McMurphy, seem "any crazier than the
average asshole on the street" (p. 63). McMurphy comes to the asylum from a prison work farm. He has been a logger, a war hero, a
gambler, and generally a happy, heavily muscled, self-made drifter
and tough guy. A contest develops between McMurphy (whose ini-
tials, R. P. M., urge us to note his power) and the Big Nurse (whose
name, Ratched, tips us off about her mechanical nature as well as
her offensive function as a "ball-cutter"). The implications of the
contest deepen; it becomes a battle pitting the individual against all
those things that make up the modern wasteland, for the Nurse represents singly what the institution and its rules really are. The drama
of the battle is intense, and the action seesaws as McMurphy gradually discovers he must give his strength to others in order to pry
loose the Big Nurse's hold on their manhood. As they gain in health,
McMurphy weakens, and his ultimate victory over the Big Nurse is
a mixed one. He is lobotomized, a "castration of the frontal lobes,"
but he gives his lifeblood to Chief Bromden who breaks free and
leaves behind in the Nurse and the Institution not a destroyed power,
but a shrunken, silent, and temporarily short-circuited one. Beauti-
fully structured, the novel provides us with both a brilliant version
of our contemporary wasteland and a successful Grail Knight, who
frees the Fisher King and the human spirit for a single symbolic and
transcendent moment of affirmation.

The world of this wasteland is mechanically controlled from a
central panel, as the narrator sees it, so that everything in it is run
by tiny electrical wires or installed machinery. People are often robots
or are made of electric tubing and wiring and springs, as the "adjusted" ones seem to be. The Big Nurse is only one agent of a "Combine" which rules all things, including time and the heart and mind

of man. *Combine*, as the word implies, is not just an organization; it is a mechanism, a machine that threshes and levels; its ends are Efficiency and Adjustment. According to Chief Bromden, the Combine had gone a long way in doing things to gain total control,

> *things like, for example—a* train *stopping at a station and laying a string of full-grown men in mirrored suits and machine hats, laying them like a hatch of identical insects, half-life things coming pht-pht-pht out of the last car, then hooting its electric whistle and moving on down the spoiled land to deposit another hatch. (p. 227–28)*

Those are the adjusted ones. The ones who cannot adjust are sent to the asylum to have things installed so that the Combine can keep them in line.

> *The ward is a factory for the Combine. It's for fixing up mistakes made in the neighborhoods and in the schools and the churches, the hospital is. When a completed product goes back out into society, all fixed up good as new,* better *than new sometimes, it brings joy to the Big Nurse's heart; something that came in all twisted different is now a functioning, adjusted component, a credit to the whole outfit and a marvel to behold. Watch him sliding across the land with a welded grin, fitting into some nice little neighborhood. (p. 38)*

He is a "Dismissal," spiritually and morally empty, but "happy" and adjusted. If you do not fit, you are a malfunctioning machine—

> *machines with flaws inside that can't be repaired, flaws born in, or flaws beat in over so many years of the guy running head-on into solid things that by the time the hospital found him he was bleeding rust in some vacant lot. (p. 4)*

That is what is called a "Chronic." Some people do escape in a way. People like McMurphy who keep moving, and people like Pete Bancini who are just too simple, are missed by the Combine, and if they are lucky, they can get hidden and stay missed.

All this is only the view of the narrator, a paranoid Indian. But there is enough evidence in the way the world around Chief Bromden runs to make his terms more and more acceptable as the novel progresses. Among the few characters on the "Outside" that Kesey takes the time to describe is one of the insulting loafers who taunt the patients while they wait to board their boat for the fishing trip. The man is described as having "purple under his eyes," the same kind of purple that appears under the eyes of all the ward's finished, lobotomized products. There is, at least for a moment, a frightening suggestion that the Combine's inmates may truly be everywhere. For Chief Bromden, it is no madman's logic—after seeing the actual persecution of his father, family, and tribe by the U.S. Department of the Interior—to posit a large central organization that seeks the doom of all things different.

The wasteland of the asylum is characterized not only by mechanization and efficiency but by sterility, hopelessness, fear, and guilt. The inmates are aimless, alienated, and bored; they long for escape; they "can connect / Nothing with Nothing," not even picture puzzles; they are enervated and emasculated; their dignity is reduced to something less than human. Most of all, they are run as the asylum is run—by women; it is a "matriarchy," and behind almost every ruined man is a grasping, castrating female whose big bosom belies her sterility but reveals a smothering momism. So, McMurphy perceives almost immediately that Big Nurse Ratched is pecking at their "everlovin' balls." But the same has been true of Harding's wife, and Chief Bromden's mother, and Billy Bibbit's mother—and these are just about the only women we see in the novel, except a couple of sweet whores named Candy and Sandy. However, what is more startling about this terrible world is its leveling sense of order and its rules. In one incident McMurphy wants to brush his beeth before the proper teeth-brushing time. He is told that the toothpaste is locked up. After questioning the aide about what possible harm anyone could do with a tube of toothpaste, he is advised that the toothpaste is locked up because it is the rule, and rules are rules. After all, what would happen if everyone just started brushing his teeth whenever he had a mind to. Kesey's point by this time is clear; the true madness, the real dry root of the wasteland is not the patient's irrationality, but the deadly order, system, and rationality of the institution. What is normal is perverted, and reason becomes madness, while some small hope for salvation lies in the nonrational if not the downright irrational.

The institution's general significance and its effect on humanity come together in the single person of the Big Nurse, who causes the patients' hopelessness, their inadequacy, fear, anxiety, and alienation. She is the institution itself, the wasteland personified. White and starched stiff, she suggests Melville's plunge into the dreadful ambiguity and possible evil that could live in the heart of what is white. (McMurphy wears fancy shorts with jumping white whales on them, given to him by an Oregon State coed who called him a "symbol.") But with the Big Nurse the ambiguity is only superficial and thrives only on the name of respectability—her real villainy is clear. She is the enemy, the "Belladonna," obstacle to the Grail Knight. She enervates her patients by playing upon their fears, guilts, and inadequacies. She and all other castrators are

> *people who try to make you weak so they can get you to toe the line, to follow their rules, to live like they want you to. And the best way to do this, to get you to knuckle under, is to weaken you by gettin' you where it hurts the worst. (p. 58)*

She is relentless in her crippling pity and capable of using any weapon in order to preserve her control. She has handpicked her aides, three shadowy and sadistic black men who are hooked to her by electrical impulses of hate. They have been twisted by white brutality, and their response is savage. As weapons in the Big Nurse's arsenal, they serve as symbols of the force of guilt, which she uses to torment her patients. Guilt and the black man twine identities in the white mind to cut deeper into its already vitiated self-respect.

The Big Nurse is continually pictured in images of frost or machinery, or as a crouching, swelling beast. She is described as a collection of inert materials: plastic, porcelain—any of modern America's favorite respectable synthetics.

> *Her face is smooth, calculated, and precision-made, like an expensive baby doll, skin like flesh-colored enamel, blend of white and cream and baby-blue eyes, small nose, pink little nostrils—everything working together except the color on her lips and fingernails, and the size of her bosom. (p. 5)*

She is sexless and cold enough to halt McMurphy's lecture on how a man can always win out over a woman; she is "impregnable" in almost every sense, even by so vaunted a "whambam" as McMurphy.

> *What she dreams of there in the center of those wires is a*
> *world of precision efficiency and tidiness like a pocket*
> *watch with a glass back, a place where the schedule is*
> *unbreakable and all the patients who aren't Outside,*
> *obedient under her beam, are wheelchair Chronics with*
> *catheter tubes run direct from every pant-leg to the sewer*
> *under the floor. (p. 17)*

She controls clock time, has all the rules on her side, and uses insinuation like a torture rack. Fear, cowardice, and timidity are all she sees in man. She sums up all that is debilitating to the individual about a modern world of massive institutions. In wasteland terms, she is the keeper of the keys, the false prophet; for not only is she the cause of enervation and divison, but she also perverts the holy words that are the key to coping with the wasteland. When she gives, she emasculates; when she sympathizes, she reduces; and when she controls, she destroys. McMurphy, the Grail Knight, the savior, not only must contest her power, but must listen to, learn how to live by, and restore the true meaning of the holy words from "What the Thunder Said": Give, Sympathize, Control.

The narrative movement of the novel is built around McMurphy's growth in knowledge and his progress toward curing Chief Bromden. As he learns to give and to sympathize, he moves toward death while the Chief moves toward rebirth, "blown-up" to full size by McMurphy's sacrifice and gift of self-control. At the beginning we are given two images foreshadowing McMurphy's fate: Ellis, the patient who stands like an empty Christ, arms outstretched in tortured crucifixion, fixed that way by an electric shock machine used as a weapon of the institution; and Ruckly, blanked of all but mindless, obscene answers and beaten by the trump card of the institution—lobotomy— beaten as a means of dealing with his rebellion. McMurphy will also be personally beaten, crucified, and lobotomized, because there is no final victory over the Big Nurse and her wasteland; she will continue just as Eliot's wasteland continues after the rain that falls.

> *She's too big to be beaten. She covers one whole side of*
> *the room like a Jap statue. There's no moving her and no*

> *help against her. She's lost a little battle here today, but*
> *it's a minor battle in a big war that she's been winning*
> *and that she'll go on winning . . . just like the Combine,*
> *because she has all the power of the Combine behind her.*
> *(p. 109)*

But the little battle she loses is enough to cure the Chief and bring a little rain to a parched land.

Ironically, McMurphy enters the asylum supposedly on a request for "transfer" to get "new blood" for his poker games, but from that very entrance, as he laughs, winks, and goes around shaking limp hands, it is he that does the transferring and the giving of blood. The first foretelling of his effect on Chief Bromden comes as McMurphy seizes the Chief's hand.

> *That palm made a scuffing sound against my hand. I*
> *remember the fingers were thick and strong closing over*
> *mine, and my hand commenced to feel peculiar and went*
> *to swelling up out there on my stick of an arm, like he*
> *was transmitting his own blood into it. It rang with*
> *blood and power. It blowed up near as big as his.*
> *(pp. 23–24).*

He brings contact, the human touch, to a place sterilized of all but inverted relationships. His giving and his sacrifice are not, however, a continuous unbroken process, but are correlated to his learning. He launches into full battle with the Big Nurse and begins pulling the patients out of their tranquilized fog. His first assault reaches its peak in the contest over TV privileges.

McMurphy strengthens the other men enough to rebel in unison against the Big Nurse, and he does it by the symbolic gesture of attempting to lift a massive "control panel." It is a symbol of his resistance and willingness to keep trying even when he is going to be beaten, even when he *knows* he is going to be beaten. The strain on him is balanced by his effect on the men and on Chief Bromden in particular. The Chief asserts himself for the first time. He raises his hand to join the vote against the Big Nurse and recognizes that no external power is controlling him—he himself has lifted his own arm expressing his own decision. This first sign of self-control, inspired by McMurphy's struggle with the control panel, leads the Chief out of his fog and out of his safety; he ceases to be the blind, impotent Tiresias and begins literally to see again. Waking up late at night, he looks out a window and sees clearly, without hallucination—something he has been unable to do since he has been in the asylum. What he sees, on another level, is that McMurphy has succeeded in being himself, that it is possible to be yourself without hiding and without the Combine getting you. But just as the Chief makes this discovery, McMurphy learns what it really means to be "committed" in this asylum, and he faces the temptation that is hazard to any Grail Knight— the temptation to quit.

Learning that most of the patients are "voluntary," that he is one of the few "committed," and that the duration of his commitment is to be determined by the Big Nurse, McMurphy becomes "cagey" (an ominous word in this mechanized world). He promptly ceases giving and ceases sympathizing. The immediate result is an assertion of the wasteland—Cheswick, one of the patients dependent on McMurphy, drowns himself. Without resistance from the Grail Knight, the wasteland perverts water, the symbol of fertility, into the medium of death.

But the demands made on McMurphy by the weaker inmates determine his return to battle, for the weak are driven to the wasteland by "Guilt. Shame. Fear. Self-belittlement" (p. 294), while the strong are driven by the needs of the weak. As the Chief ultimately realizes, McMurphy is driven by the inmates, and this drive

> had been making him go on for weeks, keeping him
> standing long after his feet and legs had given out, weeks
> of making him wink and grin and laugh and go on with
> his act long after his humor had been parched dry
> between two electrodes. (pp. 304–5).

To signal his renewed challenge to the institution and his acceptance of commitment, McMurphy stands up at what looks like the Big Nurse's decisive victory, strides mightily across the ward, "the iron in his bootheels cracking lightning out of the tile," and runs his fist through the Big Nurse's enormous glass window, shattering her dry hold as "the glass comes apart like water splashing" (p. 190). McMurphy knows where his gesture will lead; he was told in the very beginning that making trouble—breaking windows and similar actions—will lead him to crucifixion on the shock table and destruction by lobotomy.

What McMurphy has learned is the secret of "What the Thunder Said," for, as one critic of Eliot's poem explained it:

> *If we can learn to give of ourselves and to live in*
> *sympathetic identification with others, perhaps we may*
> *also learn the art of self-control and thereby prepare*
> *ourselves to take on the most difficult of responsibilities:*
> *that of giving directions ourselves, of controlling our*
> *destinies and perhaps those of others, as an expert*
> *helmsman controls a ship.* [2]

McMurphy, as helmsman, leads his twelve followers, including Chief Bromden, aboard a ship and on a fishing trip where, through his active sympathy, he gives them the gift of life so that they may gain control of their own destinies. The fishing trip—considering that fish are traditional mystical symbols of fertility—is the central incident in McMurphy's challenge to the wasteland. What he gives to the men is drained from his own lifeblood, and the path of his descent to weariness is crossed by Chief Bromden "pumped up" to full size, the cured Fisher King. And at that point, we are told "the wind was blowing a few drops of rain" (p. 294). "*Damyata:* The boat responded / Gaily, to the hand expert with sail and oar."

McMurphy gives the men not only self-confidence and a renewed sense of virility, but also what Kesey sees as man's only weapon against the wasteland—laughter. There has been no laughter in the asylum; McMurphy notices that immediately and comments, "when you lose your laugh you lose your *footing*" (p. 68). By the end of the fishing trip McMurphy has everyone laughing "because he knows you have to laugh at the things that hurt you just to keep yourself in balance, just to keep the world from running you plumb crazy" (pp. 237–38). In effect, he teaches the men to be black humorists, and it is the vision and the balance of black humor that Kesey attempts to employ as a stay against the wasteland. To Kesey, being human and having control means being able to laugh, for the rational, ordered world has done us in, and only an insurgence of energy from the irrational can break through the fear and sterility that have, para-doxically, made the world go mad. It is ultimately their laughter that the men cram down the Big Nurse's maw in their brief moment of victory.

In the final section of the book, McMurphy works with growing fatigue and resignation toward his inevitable sacrifice. He battles with the Nurse's aides, gets repeated shock treatments, has a chance to capitulate to the Big Nurse and refuses, returns from the cruelty of the shock table to the ward where he is faced with the charge of mixed and ulterior motives, and finally holds his mad vigil in the upside-down world of the Chapel Perilous. But madness here is antiorder, and so a sign of health. The scene is the night of Billy Bibbit's lost virginity. McMurphy and his followers run wild, completely subverting the order of the Big Nurse's ward and violating the sanctity of all rules. Billy's entrance into manhood symbolizes the inmates' initiation into the final mysteries of life and fertility. All this is as it should be during and following a vigil in the Chapel Perilous. But, as we already know, you cannot beat the Big Nurse. She regains her power by cowing Billy with shame and forcing him to betray his deliverer. Billy, broken again, slits his throat, and the Big Nurse attempts one last time to turn guilt against McMurphy. His response is the ultimate sacrificial gesture; he rips open her dress, exposing her mountainous and smothering breasts, and chokes her—not able to kill her, but only to weaken and silence her. The contest ends in violence, the individual's last offense against the immensities that oppress him. Kesey, like John Hawkes, finds something ultimately necessary and cleansing about violence.

At McMurphy's fall,

> he gave a *cry*. At the last, falling backward, his face
> appearing to us for a second upside down before he was
> smothered on the floor by a pile of white uniforms, he let
> himself cry out: a sound of cornered-animal fear and hate
> and surrender and defiance. (p. 305)

It was the only sound and the only sign that "he might be anything other than a sane willful, dogged man performing a hard duty" (p. 305). His madness is all the salvation the twentieth century can muster, for to give and to sympathize in our kind of wasteland is itself a sign of madness. McMurphy is lobotomized, and in the final moments of the book, Chief Bromden snuffs out the life of the body connected to that already dead spirit and, with his gift of life, seizes the huge "control panel" McMurphy had blown him up to lift, then spins it through the asylum window. "The glass splashed out in the moon, like a bright cold water baptizing the sleeping earth" (p. 310). The

Fisher King is free. Although the wasteland remains, McMurphy, the redheaded Grail Knight, has symbolically transcended it through his gesture of sacrifice, and at least allowed others to "come in under the shadow of this red rock."

One Flew Over the Cuckoo's Nest is a modern fable that pits a fabulous use of many of the traditional devices of American romance. For example, the novel emphasizes plot and action (not character), and it employs myth, allegory, and symbol. There are equally obvious points of contact between the themes of Kesey's book and traditional American themes, such as the rebellion against old orders and old hierarchies, and the need for communal effort in the face of an alien and overwhelmingly negative force. *Cuckoo's Nest* is closely tied to American tradition, yet there is much in it that offers a paradigm for what is different about the characteristic vision in the American novel of the 1960s. It does not return to the past, gaze toward the future, or travel to the unknown to get its "romance" setting. The setting is the static institution which sums up both the preoccupation of our age with the mystery of power, and the substitution of an image of the wasteland for the image of a journey between Eden and Utopia. It is shot through with the vitality of its use of the here and now. We are constantly shocked into discovering how the book is really tied to the recognizable, not to the distant or strange, but to our very own world—to the technology we know, the clichés we use, the atmosphere possible only in the atomic tension of our times. Just as no one can confidently say who is mad and who is not in Kesey's novel, no one can say in what sense his story is real and in what sense it is fiction. The narrator sounds a note that echoes everywhere in the sixties:

> *You think this is too horrible to have really happened, this*
> *is too awful to be the truth! But please. It's still hard for*
> *me to have a clear mind thinking on it. But it's the truth*
> *even if it didn't happen. (p. 8)*

The romance elements in the book are not based on devices that whisk us away to some "theatre, a little removed from the highway of ordinary travel,"[3] and then whisk us back fueled up with truth. We suspect with horror that what we are seeing very possibly *is* our highway of ordinary travel, fantastic as it may seem.

The romance elements in *One Flew Over the Cuckoo's Nest* are inspired by a world vision which questions the sanity of fact. It is a cartoon and comic-strip world—where a man's muscles can be "blown-up" like Popeye's arms after a taste of spinach—"a cartoon world, where the figures are flat and outlined in black, jerking through some kind of goofy story that might be real funny if it weren't for the cartoon figures being real guys" (p. 31). Not only is this a good image of Kesey's world, but it supplies the pattern for his character development. The movement from being a cartoon figure to becoming a painfully real guy is exemplified by Billy Bibbit. His name and his personality are reminiscent of comic-strip character Billy Batson, a little crippled kid, weak and helpless, who could say "Shazam" and turn into Captain Marvel. And just when Billy Bibbit stops being a little crippled kid, after the comic-book fun of his tumble with Candy, just when his "Whambam" Shazam should turn him into this big, powerful, unbeatable Captain Marvel, the Big Nurse turns him into a real guy—a Judas, in fact, who proceeds from betrayal to slitting his very real throat.[4] While Kesey attempts to employ the mode of black humor, and while he does see the value of laughter in coping with the wasteland, one suspects that he is more pained and embittered by the "real guy" than a black humorist can afford to be. His humor often loses that fine edge between pain and laughter that we see in Elkin, Vonnegut, Barth, and Pynchon, while his "flat" portrayal of women and of blacks is more stereotypic and uncomfortable than funny or appropriate to his cartoon-character pattern. It borders too much on the simplistic.

The romance elements also revolve around our new version of mystery. Though we may certainly be tempted to call it paranoia, it is definitely a part of the equipment of our times, and it is undoubtedly malevolent. The Big Nurse, the Combine, the asylum—all three seem to symbolize that immense power that reduces us, and that seems to be mysteriously unlocatable. Kesey is one of those writers of the sixties who explore some mystery about fact itself that portends mostly defeat for man. This sense of mystery adds complexity to the paradoxes of what is mad and sane, real and unreal, for it drives us to seek its heart in some huge force conspiring against us. Although it arises in connection with the image of the wasteland, this mystery is the antipathy of Eliot's hoped-for God. It is only a further cause of divisive fear.

The mystery is best represented, to Kesey, by the asylum itself, but he leaves us with two possible locations of the mystery's source. It could be located somewhere external to us, as Chief Bromden sees it, or, as McMurphy tries to explain, maybe blaming it on a Combine is "just passing the buck." It may really be our own "deep-down hang-up that's causing the gripes" (p. 181). Perhaps there is some big bad wolf—and then perhaps there is only us. In the past, the essential shock in American fictional experience has been a character's discovery that deep down he too is capable of evil; the shock in the sixties is the character's discovery that deep down he may be a source of unrelenting insanity. Down there, perhaps, that unknowable and seemingly immense power against us comes into being and then mounts to become a world gone mad. Against or within that shock, the writer, the prophet, sees new paradoxes of reason and irrationality, fact and mystery, and writes his novels no longer sure of what is fact or fiction, nor whether malevolence lies within or without. His only possible rationale is this one, voiced by a Kesey character:

> *These things don't happen. . . . These things are*
> *fantasies you lie awake at night dreaming up and then*
> *are afraid to tell your analyst. You're not really here.*
> *That wine isn't real; none of this exists. Now, let's go*
> *on from there. (p. 285)*

Notes

1. Ken Kesey, *One Flew Over the Cuckoo's Nest* (New York: Viking, 1962), p. 7. All subsequent references are to this edition, and are parenthesized within the text.

2. Kimon Friar and John Malcolm Brinin, eds., *Modern Poetry* (New York: Appleton-Century-Crofts, 1951), p. 472.

3. Nathaniel Hawthorne, "Preface" to *Blithedale Romance* (New York: Norton, 1958), p. 27.

4. Kesey actually refers directly to the "Captain Marvel" comic strip in a long discussion in his second novel *Sometimes a Great Notion* (New York: Viking, 1964), p. 142–43.

7

Mechanistic and Totemistic Symbolization in Kesey's *One Flew Over the Cuckoo's Nest*

●●●●●●●●●●●●●●●●

Don Kunz

In *Form and Fable in American Fiction,* Daniel G. Hoffman describes how Hawthorne and Melville transformed Puritan allegory, which was designed for the elucidation of certainties, into a symbolic method by using it in the service of search, skepticism, and sometimes a comedic affirmation of human values.[1] Of course the symbolic method characteristic of the American novel does not now depend upon Puritanism's gradual disintegration and periodic resurgence. Perhaps this technique remains current because so many of our novelists insist upon inquiring into the meaning of becoming an American in terms of a dream. In dreams, interior, subjective experience is expressed as if it were exterior and sensory. And according to Erich Fromm, "this interchange between the two modes of experience is the very essence of symbols, and particularly of the dream world."[2] Treating the shifting national Platonic conception of the self encourages symbolization. Ken Kesey is no different from other American novelists in finding

Originally published in *Studies in American Fiction* 3: 1 (1975): 65–82. Reprinted by permission.

his symbols within our cultural detritus. But in *One Flew Over the Cuckoo's Nest*, his fusion of specified conceptual sources comprises an ingeniously comprehensive symbolic matrix and gives that traditional technique new validity.

One source descends from Newton's conception of the physical world as an orderly mechanism, a view later applied by the Naturalists to animal and human behavior. Kesey's most immediate model of it is the idea of man as a reactive organism, the theory that dominated all schools of American psychology during the first half of this century, including classical and neobehaviorism, learning and motivation theories, psychoanalysis, and cybernetics.[3] The idea that man responds predictably to stimuli, is shaped by environmental conditioning, and strives in the most economic fashion to achieve homeostasis is for Kesey a nightmarish absurdity. *A priori*, these behavioral hypotheses are a sophisticated extension of classical physics. Experientially, and as an exclusive theory, the novelist sees them as a grotesque, dehumanizing myth, which receives suicidal endorsement by an America that glorifies machinery. Kesey's first novel dramatically and symbolically reduces the American psychologists' robotic theory to delusion and hallucination and, so, casts doubt upon the sanity of a nation which subscribes to it. *One Flew Over the Cuckoo's Nest* also revitalizes from an existentialist posture one of the oldest American alternative visions: totemism.

The setting is a mental hospital in Oregon after the Korean War. The narrator is a gigantic half-Indian inmate, Chief Bromden. We see him first as the victimized exemplar of his therapists' reductive mechanical theory and later as a heroic model of the vitalistic view of man. Early in the novel Bromden exhibits the usual behavioral symptoms of the schizophrenic: hallucination and delusion, confusion, stupor, and fluctuation of mood from manic to depressed.[4] Although he is ambulatory, the narrator is considered a "Chronic" case beyond therapeutic help; he feigns deafness and dumbness, avoids contact with other inmates, and sometimes feels frozen in place by a solidifying plastic, pinned down by a one-thousand-pound weight, or, more often, lost in and stupefied by a thick fog. He seems unable to control the confusing free association of memory, fantasy, and present sensory experience. He thinks of himself, his fellow inmates, and his therapists in the hospital as machines; his ward is variously imagined to be a hydroelectric dam, slaughter house, smelter, and, most often, a factory. Bromden fears that the Head Nurse and her staff are part of a vast conspiracy he calls the "Combine," an organization engaged in secret control of a nation of robots:

> She wields a sure power that extends in all directions
> on hairlike wires too small for anybody's vision but mine;
> I see her sit in the center of this web of wires like a
> watchful robot, tend her network with mechanical insect
> skill, know every second which wire runs where and just
> what current to send up to get the result she wants. . . .
>
> What she dreams of there in the center of those wires
> is a world of precision efficiency and tidiness like a pocket
> watch with a glass back, a place where the schedule is
> unbreakable, and all the patients who aren't Outside,
> obedient under her beam, are wheelchair Chronics with
> catheter tubes run direct from every pantleg to the sewer
> under the floor. . . .
>
> Efficiency locks the ward like a watchman's clock.
> Everything the guys think and say and do is all worked
> out months in advance, based on the little notes the nurse
> makes during the day. This is typed and fed into the
> machine I hear humming behind the steel door in the rear
> of the Nurse's station.[5]

In *One Flew Over the Cuckoo's Nest*, the robotic theory of man is held by therapist and patient alike. Supposedly the therapists' depersonalization of the patient is in the interest of objectivity. Yet if scientists have refused to read human intentions into the world of things or animals in the name of objectivity, why should they read animal and mechanical intentions into a world of people? Kesey compels us to see that the therapist who tries to transmute persons into efficiently adjusted social automatons is as crazy as the inmate who conceives of himself as a mechanical zombie. In fact, the therapist may be more so, since, according to existentialist psychiatrist R. D. Laing, "the behavior of the patient is to some extent a function of the behavior of the psychiatrist in the same behavioral field."[6]

The schizoid individual often pretends he is a machine engaged in a sterile but efficient interaction with other machines because he feels his own precariously structured identity would be threatened by a real, live dialectical relationship (Laing, pp. 80–101). Kesey's huge half-Indian narrator accepts a false mechanical self supplied by his therapists: he is referred to as the "soo-pah Chief" (p. 9), "Chief Broom" (p. 11), and "a six-foot-eight sweeping machine" (p. 65) so often that he comes to conceive of himself as an "arcade puppet" (p. 33) moved along the floor by powerful magnets. He reacts to his therapists as if they, too, are machines directing him by electronic cues. The Head Nurse's "face is smooth, calculated, and precision-made" (p. 11); her eyes sweep "back and forth over them as steady as a turning beacon" (p. 49); when she moves "she rumbles past . . . big as a truck" (p. 87); she carries "a bag shape of a tool box . . . full of a thousand parts she aims to use in her duties today—wheels and gears, cogs polished to a hard glitter, tiny pills that gleam like porcelain, needles, forceps, watchmaker's pliers, roles of copper wire . . ." (p. 10). Her aides are "black machinery" (p. 10), "black as telephones" (p. 32); their eyes shine out of their black faces "like the hard glitter of radio tubes" (p. 9); they are "locomotives" (p. 233)—an outrageous pun—or at best "bugs" (p. 90) or "greasemonkeys" (p. 233)—one step or two further up the great chain of being. Such a schizoid depersonalization of therapists and self is conceived not in the interest of objectivity but survival, a defensive strategy to protect the real self by the creation of a false self. The compliance of this false self with the will of others reaches an extreme form in the catatonic and hebephrenic, whose obedience, imitation, and coping are so excessive as to constitute a grotesque parody, a secret indictment of the manipulating therapist (Laing, p. 109). One of the functions of Kesey's narrator, then, is to reveal himself as both victim and mocker of his therapists' institutionalized insanity, specifically as it takes the form of a depersonalized theory of persons, a false allegory of life constructed in the interest of dispassionate scientific inquiry and control.

The chief symbol of this mass-manufactured insanity is the ubiquitous "Combine." It is Kesey's version of the psychologists' American dream adopted through environmental manipulation: mechanized learning, assembly-line production, motivation research applied in advertising through mass media. And the mental hospital is an American microcosm. The narrator tells us "the ward is a factory of the Combine. It's for fixing up mistakes made in the neighborhoods and in the schools and in the churches . . ." (p. 40). He thinks he and the other "Chronics" have been permanently recalled to avoid giving the robotic product a bad name; the "Acutes" are defective units salvageable by additional installation of controls like "the IBM Indwelling Curiosity Cutout" or by reconditioning or readjustment (pp. 19–21, 36). Flawed because out of control, these inmates represent an American minority of primitive individualists.

Of course the psychological jargon that the therapists apply to their patients is a vocabulary of denigration. Like the existentialist psychiatrists Van den Berg and Laing, Kesey deplores this tendency to speak of psychosis as a social or biological failure to adjust because it implies a certain standard way of being human to which the psychotic cannot measure up. Such a language is "the outcome of efforts to avoid thinking in terms of freedom, choice, responsibility" (Laing, p. 27). And like Hawthorne and Melville, Kesey transforms the allegorical method sanctioned by a disintegrating ideal—in this case psychological rather than theological—while he challenges the certainty of its truths. He makes the robotic allegory of man a source of symbol in the service of search, skepticism, and comedic affirmation of human values. The mechanical symbols turned back upon the therapists who are ultimately responsible for them renders them comic, according to Henri Bergson's well-known definition: we laugh at them because they are human beings declined from a vitalistic ideal.[7] But our laughter is more sympathetic toward the inmates. They are the artists of parody and mimicry whom we would laugh at, rather than with, for acting out their prescribed "therapeutic roles" like cartoon figures if we did not see them as real people behind the symptoms of their psychotic illness. The patients are comic heroes trying to survive a socially approved sacrifice of the self.

Bromden's schizophrenic vision is too terrifying, vivid, and convincingly ingenious to make him contemptible.The schizophrenia itself makes him a fascinating personality, literally many-faceted. And the complicated vignettes by which his case history is gradually revealed create powerful insights into the experience of becoming an American. His father, "the-Pine-That-Stands-Tallest-on-the-Mountain," was a huge Chief of a now defunct tribe of Columbia Gorge Indians, his mother a white woman whose marriage to the Chief was the harbinger of further white, "civilized" encroachments upon the primitive world of the American native son (p. 186). And after encroachment came assimilation or extermination—biracial sides of the same coin. The U.S. Department of the Interior forced the Chief to sell the tribal fishing rights to the Columbia Falls where it constructed a hydroelectric dam with Indian labor. Because the tribal culture, its identity, centered around fishing, the Chief complained that no monetary compensation was adequate. But he was given no alternative. After this compulsory participation in self-destruction, he experienced loss of vision, confusion, and the feeling that he had dwindled in size—the schizophrenic symptoms that his narrator-son partly inherits, partly is conditioned to accept in a new culture.

This psychological phenomenon of socially induced reduction was followed to its logical conclusion as the tribe became defunct, Vanishing Americans. For the Chief the process had been hastened by adopting his wife's name of Bromden because "that name makes gettin' that Social Security card a lot easier" (p. 239) when they move to town. While the Chief shrunk through brainwashing, his wife seemed to grow in stature, as she dominated the marriage and presided over the decline of the tribe. Thus, the narrator's mother symbolizes the incursion into and emasculation of the Native American population by the white, immigrant civilization.[8] This white, urban, matriarchal, European domination of the red, rural, masculine, native culture culminates in a standardized, homeostatic society. And whatever cultural dualism lingers in mental institutions translates at the personal level into schizophrenia. Kesey's narrator is the archetypal American: half red native, half white immigrant; half-committed to the disappearing wilderness, half-mesmerized by the siren sounds of urban civilization. He is the defective product of the emasculated father and the castrating mother. He is literally and symbolically the split personality which Eugen Bleuler had in mind when he coined the name for the symptomatic disorder *schizophrenia*, derived from the Greek *schizein* for split and *phren* for mind (Jackson, p. 65).

That side of the narrator identified with the white culture legitimizes his acceptance of the conceptual framework of early twentieth-century American psychologists. He has been conditioned to accept a robotic view of himself and others, beginning at the family level. In fact his hallucinated association of the hydroelectric dam with the hospital/factory makes the psychiatric ward the historical extension of the Department of the *Interior*; it continues to eliminate systematically those it defines as social misfits according to its theory of adjustment. The ward nurse, Miss Ratched, *Big* Nurse, becomes an institutionalized surrogate matriarch who reconditions the native sons. But the fact that the narrator is half Indian also makes available an

opposing conceptual source for symbolic exploitation: native totemism. And it is from this second idea-set, in which Kesey sees existentialist possibilities, that he devises a more humanistic self-image,
language, and world view for the American.

When the narrator is able to suppress his false, mechanical image,
his real self conceives of the world more "primitively":

> *I hide in the mop closet and listen, my heart beating
> in the dark, and I try to keep from getting scared, try to
> get my thoughts off someplace else—try to think back and
> remember things about the village and the big Columbia
> River, think about ah one time Papa and me were
> hunting birds in a stand of cedar trees near The Dalles.
> . . . But like always when I try to place my thoughts in
> the past and hide there, the fear close at hand seeps in
> through the memory. I can feel that least black boy out
> there coming up the hall, smelling out for my fear. He
> opens out his nostrils like black funnels, his outsized head
> bobbing this way and that as he sniffs, and he sucks in
> fear from all over the ward. He's smelling and he's
> hunting around. I try to keep still. . . .*
>
> *(Papa tells me to keep still, tells me that the dog
> senses a bird somewheres right close. . . . The bird safe as
> long as he keeps still. . . . Then the bird breaks, feathers
> springing, jumps out of the cedar into the birdshot from
> Papa's gun.)*
>
> *The least black boy and one of the bigger ones catch
> me before I get ten steps out of the mop closet. . . .*
> (pp. 12–13)

The passage reveals that the schizophrenic cannot rely upon memory
to sustain a vitalistic sense of being-in-the-world (bird, dog, hunter);
it is too often fearfully suppressed by the mechanistic world view of
the controlling therapist (nostrils like black funnels, sucks in fear).
The narrator's self observes and judges its image as the image begins
to assume the characteristics of the false self more and more, to the
point of self-destruction: he declines from hunting man to hunted
and dead bird to refuse sucked from the closet by the vacuum-cleaner
aide. If Chief Bromden cannot find some way to protect the true self-
image from external control, he will define himself more and more

according to the false, mechanical self designed by the Combine. In one sense, he becomes a suicide; in another, he is legally and sophisticatedly murdered by his therapists.

The Indian side of the narrator's personality, the constantly threatened, vital, true self is dramatically sustained by the appearance of R. P. McMurphy—logger, gambler, Korean War hero with a dishonorable discharge, a record of convictions for assault and battery, and an indictment for statutory rape. McMurphy has feigned psychopathy in order to escape the drudgery of hoeing peas on the prison work farm and to find a new group of "suckers" for his con games. The schizophrenic narrator sensitively interprets McMurphy as a white Indian, a primitive American individualist. One half of the narrator thinks of McMurphy mechanically:

> Maybe he growed up so wild all over the country, batting
> around from one place to another, never around one town
> longer'n a few months when he was a kid so a school
> never got much a hold on him, logging, gambling,
> running carnival wheels, traveling lightfooted and fast,
> keeping on the move so much that the Combine never had
> a chance to get anything installed. (p. 84)

But the other half sees him vitalistically, mythically:

> He sounds like he's way above them, talking down, like
> he's sailing fifty yards overhead, hollering at those below
> on the ground. He sounds big. I hear him coming down
> the hall, and he sounds big in the way he walks, and he
> sure don't slide; he's got iron on his heels and he rings it
> on the floor like horseshoes. He shows up in the door and
> stops and hitches his thumbs in his pockets, boots wide
> apart, and stands there with the guys looking at him.
> . . . He talks a little the way Papa used to, voice loud
> and full of hell. . . . (p. 16)

Later when the half-breed narrator is more fully restored to mental health, he reveals what he had been groping toward symbolically from McMurphy's first appearance: "I still had my own notions— how McMurphy was a giant come out of the sky to save us from the Combine that was networking the land with copper wire and crystal, how he was too big to be bothered with something as measly as money . . ." (p. 224). Chief Bromden's native or true self conceives of McMurphy in terms of a fundamental myth of his vanishing culture—that a hero will appear and lead the Indian to a paradise based upon the old lifestyle. His belief in such a myth is given further credibility by the process of acculturation that he has undergone, symbolized by his half-breed status. This messianic faith is really an articulation of the Indian's spiritual depression, which is characterized by confusion, the inability to adjust to the new social environment, the undermining of old cultural norms by the white culture, disorientation, the frustration of expectation, and the loss of a foundation for security. According to Harvard anthropologist Bernard Barber:

> at such a time, messianic prophecies are most likely to be
> accepted and made the basis of action. Messiahs preach
> the return to the old order or rather, to a new order in
> which the old will be revived. Essentially, their function
> is to proclaim a stable order, one which will define the
> ends of action. Their doctrines describe men's former life,
> meaningful and satisfactory.[9]

The myth, then, is also a declaration of faith in a meaningful future.

Ordinarily, though, whites are excluded from this golden age less as a reflection of hostility toward them, than as a symbolization of the fulfillment of the former way of life. And McMurphy is white. Kesey solves this problem of integrity by means of the narrator's partial and temporary identification of McMurphy as a father figure and McMurphy's ultimate exclusion from the paradise he brings. The myth forecasts McMurphy's death as surely as his Wild Bill Hickok tattoo of Aces and Eights. It also foretells the fate of the half-breed, schizophrenic narrator: he will be cured by going fully native. The redemption of the narrator, the archetypal American, is to be accomplished by McMurphy's countertherapy, a battle and sacrifice against the forces of control symbolized by Miss Ratched, Big Nurse.

McMurphy's conception of man is vitalistic. Within minutes of his arrival on the ward he has replaced Harding as Chairman of the Patients' Council, dynamically retitled that office the "Bull Goose Loony," and begun to revitalize the robots with his language and touch. After observing a group therapy session led by Big Nurse and after hearing Doctor Spivey's explanation of "the theory of the Therapeutic Community," which aims at adjusting misfits until they "measure up" (p. 48), McMurphy offers his own analysis: it reminds him of a suicidal "peckin' party" by a "flock of dirty chickens" (pp. 55–59). And as the patients accept their new leader's assessment of their situation, they become a "society of disaffiliates" bound by a common concept of the self as unique.[10]

The primitive analogy of the pecking party assumes a symbolic and magical character as the inmates begin to think of themselves as animals rather than machines. Through Chief Bromden's eyes, we see them search for a totem, an emblem that will express the social solidarity of clanmates and define past and future meaningfully. Harding suggests they are rabbits kept in their place by a wolf/nurse. But this symbol is unsatisfactory because most of the inmates are sexually inadequate, figuratively castrated by the matriarchal civilizer who eliminates all aggressive tendencies; in part they are already machines. But in time, McMurphy's reference to himself as the "Bull Goose Loony," his comparison of the encounter session to a "peckin' party," his recurrent addressing of the inmates as "you birds," his allusion to Big Nurse as "an old Buzzard," and his habit of "goosing" the patients into asserting themselves—all this establishes a bird totem (pp. 66–67, 92).

This totemic identity is specific but various. The inmates are alternately chickens, loons, black birds, seagulls, or cormorants; McMurphy is associated with loon, goose, and even the Indian's legendary birds of power—the raven and the thunderbird. This variety allows Kesey to portray symbolically a more sophisticated set of changes within the inmates: the cowardice of the chicken, the self-conscious lunacy of the loon, the predatory nature of the cormorant, the self-sacrificing folly of the goose, the restorative power of the raven and thunderbird. Such a multiplicity of kinds within the same family also emphasizes the individuality within this society of disaffiliates and its comprehensive lineage in a primitive or restored American culture.

Soon after deciding upon a totem, McMurphy discovers most of the patients are voluntary rather than committed. In terms of their new identity, they can occasionally think of themselves as "tough birds," but they do not have "guts" (pp. 75, 123–34, 168). They are willing to join a conspiracy challenging the Nurse's policy about the television schedule, but they don't have the courage to have themselves released from the institution—to fulfill the bird's nature, which is flight. So McMurphy arranges further countertherapy to give their totem validity. Through his cure, they gain confident and responsible self-control and destroy the robotic image with which they have been indoctrinated.

One of the most important therapeutic episodes is a salmon fishing trip under the dual sponsorship of one of McMurphy's friends (a prostitute named Candy) and the ward psychiatrist, Doctor Spivey (a man who is almost more patient than therapist). As they leave the hospital,

> *a thin breeze worked at sawing what leaves were left from the oak trees, stacking them neatly against the wire cyclone fence. There was little brown birds occasionally on the fence; when a puff of leaves would hit the fence the birds would fly off with the wind. It looked at first like the leaves were hitting the fence and turning into birds and flying away. (p. 199)*

When they arrive at the coast, the patients discover McMurphy has chartered a boat called *The Lark* (p. 205). On the sea,

> *the only noise was the engine sputtering and humming, off and on, as the swells dipped the exhaust in and out of the water, and the funny, lost cry of the raggedy little black birds swimming around asking one another directions. (p. 208)*

And when Billy Bibbitt, the stutterer, hauls in "some awful thing that looked like a ten-pound toad with spines on it like a porcupine," Scanlon and the others learn "it isn't a b-b-bird" (p. 209); the totem is distinguished from its prey, and so the possibility of self-destruction becomes more remote. Then Rub-a-Dub George, the pilot, sees a flock of cormorants feeding on candle fish and drives the boat into them because that is where the salmon will be feeding, too. Here, in a moment of vitalistic chaos, the bird-men exorcize the devilish machinery implanted in them by the new culture, freeing themselves from the nightmarish vision of the psychiatrist. It constitutes a temporary regeneration of virility and self-sustaining aggression—a combination of fertility rite, sacrifice, and return to a happy hunting ground. The prostitute-sponsor, with the fishing pole scissored in her crotch, stops the reel crank, which is knocking her jacket open, with the pressure of her bare breast. Watching her, George runs the boat into a log and kills the engine. Then McMurphy confirms the more secure totemic identity, which binds the patients together as a society of misfits: "McMurphy tied a chunk of meat to each end of a four-foot string, tossed it in the air, and sent two squawking birds wheeling off, 'Till death do them part'" (p. 212).

Two other major acts of countertherapy follow. During the cleanup after the fishing trip, a black aide named Washington tortures Rub-a-Dub George, who fears dirt. Washington squirts a vile chemical wash from a tube and smears it on George with his "black! filthy! stinkin'! hand" (p. 229). McMurphy stops the torture by fighting Washington. During the battle, the patients in the shower turn into "a yellow circle, limbs and bodies knitting in a ring of flesh" (p. 230) and Chief Bromden joins in the brawl. It is a victory for the clanmates, but it is also a sacrifice for McMurphy and the narrator, who are punished with shock therapy for defending themselves and their primitive counterculture.

The next curative episode is a 2:00 A.M. ward orgy. McMurphy has two prostitute friends, Candy and Sandy, admitted through the window by the night aide, in the interest of carrying on some Masters-and-Johnson-like therapy for Billy Bibbitt, the inmate who has stuttered ever since his first word, "m-m-m-m-mama" (p. 119). But others share the panacea too: cough syrup spiked with vodka and port wine, wheelchair races up and down the halls, pot smoking, file rifling, pill throwing, and sex. Here Henry Adams' "Virgin and the Dynamo" is translated into modern comic idiom as the "Whore and the Combine": the sexual power of the Virgin is transmuted by the alchemy of absurdity into the orgasmic twitch of the whore with the heart of gold. It is a revitalization of the frontier golden age, a carnival where the life force of misrule prevails over robotic equilibrium. And the patients are equal to the cure. After Sefelt goes into one of his epileptic seizures during intercourse with Sandy, she looks down at him:

> "I never experienced anything like it," she said with quiet
> awe. . . . Sefelt didn't open his eyes, but raised a limp
> hand and picked the wallet out of his mouth. He grinned
> through his spit. "I'm all right," he said. "Medicate me
> and turn me loose again." (p. 254)

The cash nexus, if not dissolved, is at least dampened by saliva and admiration; the convulsion of the epileptic outcast is not tranquilized safely out of existence, but only medicated into a new virility and the freedom of the copulative flight.

The comic wedding march of the virginal, stuttering Billy and Candy, the whore, through an arch of flashlight beams into the Seclusion Room closely follows the mock burial of Sefelt and Sandy under a shower of tranquilizers. These ceremonies of death and resurrection, during which Billy Bibbitt's verbal twitch is replaced by a broad grin and an open fly, confirm the inmates' gradual realization that the Combine and Big Nurse, who sits at one of its control panels, are not omnipotent. The patients ally with the life force, taking on the power of the twitch embodied by the whore who earlier sponsored their fishing trip; her entrance into the ward had been a demonstration of strength:

> There was a blue smoke hung near the ceiling over her
> head; I think apparatus burned out all over the ward
> trying to adjust to her come busting in like she did—took
> electronic readings on her and calculated they weren't
> built to handle something like this on the ward, and just
> burned out, like machines committing suicide.
> (pp. 196–97)

But the cure for some of the inmates is tenuous. On the morning of the orgy, Big Nurse discovers Billy and Candy still embracing in the Seclusion Room, and Billy's stutter is quickly restored when she plays the familiar dissonant chords upon the organ of his fears. In a moment of panic and shame, he cuts his throat in the doctor's office, where he has been sent to await punishment.

The narrator's recovery is more secure; it can be measured by his steady acceptance of animal imagery for himself and the other inmates, while he continues to depersonalize the therapists with machine images. He has a vision one night of a goose leading his flock across the face of the moon, and he associates it with the honking sound made to call him out of a fog laid down over an airfield where he served during the war, as well as with McMurphy's attempts to draw him out of the fog supposedly laid down through the ventilators in the mental hospital. To emerge from this obscuring fog is to become vulnerable but clearer in his perception of the possibilities of a meaningful existence. Later, on the fishing trip, he makes a further flight beyond lunacy toward a more humanistic world view; he is able to ascend into the spirit of the bird when his self-image is secure enough to allow laughter:[11]

> It started slow and pumped itself full, swelling the men
> bigger and bigger. I watched, part of them, laughing with
> them—and somehow not with them. I was off the boat,
> blown up off the water and skating the wind with those
> black birds, high above myself, and I could look down and
> see myself and the rest of the guys, see the boat rocking
> there in the middle of those diving birds, see McMurphy
> surrounded by his dozen people, and watch them, us,
> swinging a laughter that rang out on the water in ever-
> widening circles, farther and farther, until it crashed up
> on beaches all over the coast, on beaches all over all
> coasts, in wave after wave after wave. (p. 212).

With his sense of size and will to fight restored, the narrator is able to join McMurphy in battling the forces of mechanical conditioning. As he emerges from shock therapy meted out as punishment for the shower-room brawl, Chief Bromden is able to pull memory and present experience together. According to existentialist psychologist Rollo May, such time binding signals the approach of sanity, the acquisition of the will to make existence meaningful, and a commitment to the future.[12] Bromden has the power to make the machine-induced hallucination figuratively coherent and vows never to slip off into the fog again.

It is possible that this set of dream images experienced during shock therapy accidentally simulates a kind of vision quest, which was the North American Indian's ritualistic means of acquiring supernatural power through contact with a guardian spirit.[13] But at the least, it is certain that the coherent vision signals the end of the narrator's schizophrenia and his restored, active membership in the society of American misfits. The story of Chief Bromden's gradual growth to sanity is the record of his accepting the totemic identity of the bird and the guardian spirit embodied in McMurphy as the Bull Goose Loony.

Conversely, McMurphy's transformation into the sacrificed Messiah is observed as a loss of the vitalistic symbols he brings. His title indicates that he is the bearer of a dual lineage. He is the "stud to handle the job," one who "yells like a bull," a "bull-thrower," "bull-headed," and the bull in the fight, the "fighting leatherneck" (pp. 166, 71, 201, 223, 77). But he also has "no more sensitivity than a goose," "gooses" the inmates into healthy aggression, and is the third goose of the nursery-rhyme trinity: "one flew east, one flew west, one flew over the cuckoo's nest" (pp. 56, 92, 97, 25, 239). He is loony by self-definition. Moreover, by a Christian extension of this totemistic system, he is the fisher of men who leads twelve disciples toward the coast and the regenerative sea voyage; he stands tall in his shorts, "coal black satin covered with big white whales with red eyes" (p. 76)—given to him by a coed literary major at Oregon State, along with the information that he is a symbol. By his own reckoning he is the whale among "the suckers" (p. 72), then the biggest sucker of them all, "the conman conned" (p. 166)—the poor fish who is consumed by the birds he creates and sacrificed by those he saves.

McMurphy, then, is the Indian's mythical guardian spirit that resides in the animals of air, land, and sea. He fulfills a combination of Indian and Christian messianic myths, but the Indian symbolic context dominates the narrator's interpretation of McMurphy's sacrifice as one sign that the sacrifice completes the cure, that Bromden's world view is ultimately integrated. McMurphy is seen only briefly in Christian terms: his trial on the Disturbed Ward is presided over by a robot who repeats again and again, "I wash my hands of the whole deal"; he is punished upon a cross-shaped electroshock-therapy table, his head anointed with graphite conductant and circled by "a crown of silver thorns" (pp. 232, 234, 237). He is developed more fully as the Indian cultural hero, the Creator and the Changer. According to Ella E. Clark on *Indian Legends of the Pacific Northwest*, among most of the Puget Sound and Pacific Coast tribes

> the Changer was a manlike being with supernatural
> powers. Not only could he change himself into any form
> he wished, but he transformed the creatures of the
> mythologic age into animals, birds, fishes, stars, rocks,
> and trees, in preparation for the race of human beings he
> was planning to create.[14]

Like this Creator-Changer myth, the totem poles of the Pacific Northwest, with their various combinations of bird and fish (raven and bullhead, raven and whale, the raven-finned blackfish, the eagle and blackfish, the thunderbird and the whale),[15] legitimize a multiple lineage for McMurphy as the Indian Messiah.

The pervasive totemic imagery, with which Bromden struggles to re-create his sense of being in a meaningful world, develops fragmented and overlapping versions of Pacific Northwest Indian legends. Two Quillayute legends record the presence of the guardian spirit dwelling in a thunderbird on the tallest mountain. In one, the thunderbird battles with a whale that represents evil; in another, he kills the whale with lightning and drops it in the middle of the Indian camp as an offering of food. In both, he is the tribe's savior (Clark, pp. 160–61). McMurphy is associated with the thunderbird through his massive strength, his striking like lightning with the steel taps on his heels, his thunderous voice, his similarity to the narrator's father (the-Pine-That-Stands-Tallest-on-the-Mountain), and his prolonged struggle against the white mammalian Big Nurse. But McMurphy is also associated with the great white whale as the coed's gift indicates. He is Messiah and sacrifice.

As McMurphy fulfills the messianic myth, his self-image alters inexorably from totemistic to mechanistic. The shock treatments "charge his battery," and make him the "ten-thousand-watt psychopath"; he gets his "plugs checked and points cleaned"; he thinks he may turn into a television set that will be able "to pick up channel eight" (pp. 242–44). He becomes a "Big Mack," again like the diesel truck image of his destroyer, Big Nurse, and he gives up the title of "Bull Goose Loony" to Harding when he knows the inmates are men again (p. 258). We understand Randle Patrick McMurphy, reduced by robotic therapy, is R.P.M., revolutions per minute. Finally, after the lobotomy, his eyes are "like smudged fuses in a fuse box" (p. 270). His sacrifice is a mechanically deterministic attempted rape-murder, life-death struggle with Big Nurse:

> We couldn't stop him because we were the ones
> making him do it. It wasn't the nurse that was making
> him push himself slowly up from sitting, his big hands
> driving down on the leather chair arms, pushing him up,
> rising and standing like one of those moving-picture
> zombies, obeying orders beamed at him from forty
> masters. It was us that had been making him go on for

> *weeks, keeping him standing long after his feet and legs*
> *had given out, weeks of making him wink and grin and*
> *laugh and go on with his act long after his humor had*
> *been parched dry between two electrodes.*
>
> *We made him stand and hitch up his black shorts like*
> *they were horsehide chaps, and push back his cap with*
> *one finger like it was a ten-gallon Stetson, slow,*
> *mechanical gestures—and when he walked across the floor*
> *you could hear the iron in his bare heels ring sparks out*
> *of the tile. (p. 267)*

This is a grotesque and deathly mating of two machines whose motive force is group need. As McMurphy rips her uniform, exposes her overdeveloped breasts, and assumes the missionary position with hands around her throat, he forces Big Nurse to undergo a comic mortification. In one sense it marks the symbolic death of the matriarchal castrator, the monstrous goddess of mechanical conditioning: she will never regain control over her ward. But simultaneously McMurphy has resigned himself as a "dedicated lover" (p. 218) to the tragic social catastrophe, a pre–frontal lobotomy/castration. As Harding prophecied, he is "tranquilized out of existence" (p. 255) for failure to adjust.

But it is the more productive of two deathly choices. After wagering with the inmates that he can drive Big Nurse at least temporarily crazy before she can condition him, McMurphy learns from the lifeguard at the pool the difference between being sentenced to the workfarm and committed to the mental hospital. His release, which would be a saving of life but a loss of self and of meaningful existence, depends upon becoming the robot of Miss Ratched, and the rest of the inmates, having seen the strongest among them fall, would be doomed to the same fate. But by committing himself to the patients' regeneration, McMurphy's sacrifice of identity as a frontier hero, a man out of control, might restore meaning to this absurd world. He takes the second choice, the crazy lifeguard's advice to play "guts ball" (p. 236), a term that carries life-force echoes of courage and will, as well as amplifies the sexual overtones by which the struggle is defined. Now his contest with Big Nurse becomes more than the self-interested bet, the selfish motivation which has traditionally prompted the American hero to opt out of social entanglements; he becomes the inmates' champion by subjecting himself to a rational, methodical destruction of Miss Ratched's turn-of-the-screw, popular-mechanics version of sanity. And in using self-control to become socially effective on the ward, McMurphy wills the destruction of his identity as the totally free man, the quasi-immortal frontier hero who survives an endless succession of comic episodes. By his existentialist choice of the more primitively social, regenerative, responsible of two institutional fates, he makes freedom meaningful.

When McMurphy is returned to the ward after the lobotomy, he is seen as a vegetable, "a crummy side-show fake," an "it" that Miss Ratched will use for twenty or thirty years as an example of "what can happen if you buck the system" (pp. 269–70). But in a more potent imitation of McMurphy's assault on the Nurse, Chief Bromden lies full length on top of McMurphy and smothers him. This second sacrifice insures the validity of the first. Bromden's act frees him of the robotic image which his white father-figure had assumed. The half-breed narrator can now go fully native under the aegis of his Guardian Spirit. So in a demonstration of his restored six-foot-eight-inch, two-hundred-eighty-pound identity, Chief Bromden throws the quarter-ton control panel through the glass and chickenwire window and soars birdlike out of the hospital, cured. "I felt like I was flying. Free" (p. 272).

Such a magical renaissance of the red totemistic culture and complementary decline of the white mechanistic one may seem no more than naively romantic, old-fashioned pastoral, leavened by a clever *reductio ad absurdum* of early twentieth-century American psychology—American dream and nightmare juxtaposed. Yet the symbolic nature of Chief Bromden's definition of America makes it extraordinarily effective. This is so partly because the novel is Bromden's extended hallucination, a vision quest, and partly because, as we have seen, Kesey's view of man is modern existential, as well as old country and western. His indictment of mechanism and revitalization of totemism from an existentialist posture are intimately related to his dependence upon symbolization.

Existentialist psychologists assert that as a rule mental aberrations in man (including schizophrenia) involve disturbances of symbolic functions. Since symbolization is the unique criterion of man, rat or machine models (represented here by Nurse Ratched—rat-shed, ratchet) are inadequate for understanding many neuroses.[16] In existentialist theory, mental illness may originate from a conflict between biological drives and a symbolic value system (Von Bertalanffy, p. 217); in *Cuckoo's Nest* we observe the recurrent conflict between the inmates' sexual drive and the societally imposed, mechanical self-image. Or the mental disturbance may arise from a conflict between symbolic universes or from a loss of value-orientation and the experience of meaninglessness (Von Bertalanffy, p. 217). In the novel, the narrator's loss of the masculine, rural, tribal culture and its replacement by the feminine, urban, standardized one precipitates his schizophrenia; the reversal of this acculturation effects his cure. And both the loss and restoration of Chief Bromden's sense of being-in-the-world are accomplished in the symbolic struggle between mechanistic and totemistic self-definition. Since his schizophrenia is existential, the cure is logotherapy, therapy at the symbolic level designed to stimulate what existentialist psychiatrist Viktor Frankl calls "the will-to-meaning" (*Death Camp*, pp. 101–3).

The inmates' acceptance of the bird totem is the beginning of their treatment. This does not mean that they trade robotic behavior for the animal's conditioned or instinctive activity; this would only exchange one stimulus-response scheme for another, one reductive behavioral self-image for another. Instead they use the bird as a symbol of a new spiritual, rather than a biological, identity. The totemic self-concept allows them to soar above and eventually to escape the hospital and the mechanistic theory in which they have been entrapped. They begin to imitate the sense of direction that the animal possesses through instinct, but that man must acquire through will.[17] But it is the ability to use symbols that, in itself, restores the patients to fully human status. Symbolization, that unique criterion of man, allows the inmates to transcend present experience and past conditioning in the hospital (society), to rise above "a provisional existence of unknown duration," a death-camp state of being without future or goal, a state of continuous threat of self-annihilation through perfect adjustment to a controlled environment (Frankl, *Death Camp*, p. 70). They begin to think in terms of the possible, to will their lives to have meaning. They discard the ideal of conditioning toward homeostasis for the ideal of individual responsibility through their suffering (Big Nurse's therapy), their resistance (McMurphy's countertherapy), and their experience of a value (McMurphy's sacrifice).[18]

Thus, Kesey's symbols are not just ornamental or emphatic. Symbolization constitutes what, how, and why *Cuckoo's Nest* means, an extraordinary example of technique as discovery.[19] The narrative as a gradually coherent series of hallucinations legitimizes this highly figurative language and the experiential logic of the dream so that east and west are the same direction, past and future are now, and insane therapists reinforce madness with modern techniques, while patients cure themselves with primitive word magic—and all this, in Bromden's words, is "the truth even if it didn't happen" (p. 13). Moreover, because the experiential mode of thought and concentrated symbolic language are characteristic of psychoses and primitive thinking, as well as dreaming (Fromm, p. 3), Kesey's creation of a half-Indian schizophrenic narrator undergoing existentialist logotherapy makes the symbols' dynamic function in the plot perfectly realistic. Certainly one of Kesey's finest achievements has been to surmount what Ian Watt calls the central problem of the novel: "how to impose a coherent moral structure on narrative without detracting from its air of literal authenticity."[20]

Kesey's other major achievement in this novel has been to make that coherent moral structure so comprehensive of the American experience. His existentialist *reductio ad absurdum* of the mechanistic and revitalization of the totemistic world views define the American at either end of the historical continuum. *One Flew Over the Cuckoo's Nest* measures the entropic, closed society we fear becoming against the dynamic, open society we dream of being.

Notes

1. Daniel G. Hoffman, *Form and Fable in American Fiction* (New York: Oxford University Press, 1981), p. 5.

2. Erich Fromm, "The Nature of Dreams," *Scientific American*, May 1949, p. 45.

3. Ludwig Von Bertalanffy, *General System Theory* (New York: George Braziller, 1968), pp. 205, 188–97.

4. Don D. Jackson, "Schizophrenia," *Scientific American*, Aug. 1962, p. 65.

5. Ken Kesey, *One Flew Over the Cuckoo's Nest* (1962; rpt. New York: Signet Books), pp. 30–32. All subsequent references are to this edition.

6. R. D. Laing, *The Divided Self* (1960; rpt. New York: Random House, Inc., 1969), p. 28.

7. Henri Bergson, "Laughter," in *Comedy,* ed. Wylie Sypher (Garden City, New York: Doubleday and Co., Inc., 1956), pp. 78–80.

8. In this sense the novel is an archetypal American Western according to Leslie Fiedler, *The Return of the Vanishing American* (New York: Stein and Day, 1968), pp. 24–25.

9. Bernard Barber, "Acculturation and Messianic Movements," *American Sociological Review* 6 (1941), pp. 663–65.

10. Joseph Waldmeir, "Two Novelists of the Absurd: Heller and Kesey," *Wisconsin Studies in Contemporary Literature* 5 (1964), p. 198.

11. "The neurotic who learns to laugh at himself may be on the way to self management perhaps to cure." Gordon W. Allport, *The Individual and His Religion* (New York: The Macmillan Co., 1950), p. 92.

12. Rollo May, "Contributions of Existential Psychotherapy," in *Existence: A New Dimension in Psychiatry and Psychology,* eds. Rollo May, Ernest Angel, Henri F. Ellenberger (New York: Basic Books, Inc., 1958), pp. 69–70.

13. See Robert H. Lowie, *Indians of the Plains* (New York: McGraw-Hill Book Co., Inc., 1954), pp. 157–61.

14. Ella E. Clark, *Indian Legends of the Pacific Northwest* (Berkeley: University of California Press, 1963), p. 82.

15. Viola E. Garfield and Linn A. Forrest, *The Wolf and the Raven: Totem Poles of Southeastern Alaska* (Seattle: University of Washington Press, 1948), pp. 94, 102, 126, 128.

16. Viktor E. Frankl, *From Death Camp to Existentialism: A Psychiatrist's Path to a New Therapy,* trans. Ilse Lasch (Boston: Beacon Press, 1959), p. 102; Von Bertalanffy, *General System Theory,* pp. 216–19.

17. Joseph B. Fabry, *The Pursuit of Meaning: Logotherapy Applied to Life* (Boston: Beacon Press, 1968), p. 99.

18. Viktor E. Frankl, *Man's Search for Meaning: An Introductioon to Logotherapy,* trans. Ilse Lasch (Boston: Beacon Press, 1962), p. 113; Fabry, *The Pursuit of Meaning,* p. 144.

19. See Mark Schorer, "Technique as Discovery," in *Forms of Modern Fiction: Essays Collected in Honor of Joseph Warren Bech,* ed. William Van O'Conner (Minneapolis: University of Minnesota Press, 1948), pp. 9–29.

20. Ian Watt, *The Rise of the Novel* (1957; rpt. Berkeley: University of California Press, 1967), p. 117.

8

Christ in the Cuckoo's Nest: or, the Gospel According to Ken Kesey

■■■■■■■■■■■■■■■■

Bruce E. Wallis

Considering the striking resemblances between the protagonist's actions in *One Flew Over the Cuckoo's Nest* and Mr. Kesey's own subsequent activities as head of the Merry Pranksters—activities vividly re-created in Tom Wolfe's *The Electric Kool-Aid Acid Test*—it is a profitable exercise to reinvestigate the fiction with an eye to determining its precise relationship to the fact. What such an examination reveals is a peculiarly Wildean instance of nature imitating art, for the author seems to have presented in his novel a fictional program of action, which he thereafter attempted to translate into reality. To suggest, however, that the novelist's ensuing activities were prompted simply by afterthought about his artistic creation is to understate the profound seriousness of the novel's original intentions, for despite its persistently comic spirit, the novel is expressly formulated as nothing less than the bible for a twentieth-century religion of self-assertive action, with a message of salvation modulated to the needs of repressed individuals in a constrictively conformist society.

The novel is replete with specific comparisons of McMurphy to Christ, references designed to elevate the protagonist's martyrdom

Originally published in *Cithara* 12: 1 (1972), pp. 52–58. Reprinted by permission.

to a high level of significance. But the novel is also integrated by a sustained Biblical analogy, of which these comparisons are only a part, that begins as a series of unobtrusive allusions in the early chapters, intensifies in the novel's third section (the fishing trip), and completely dominates its conclusion. The analogy compares Mc-Murphy to Christ not merely in terms of their martyrdoms, but more extensively in terms of some of the principal figures and events in the life of each. By doing so, it enables the novel to assume the configurations of a gospel, which, like the original Gospels, may serve as a source of inspiration for emulative and redemptive action.

The analogy is first struck in the third chapter, when McMurphy encounters the ward inmate Ellis, "nailed against the wall in the same condition they lifted him off the [shock shop] table for the last time, in the same shape, arms out, palms cupped."[1] Ellis's cruciform figure recurs a few pages later, where, in attempting to move, he has "the nails pull his hands back to the wall" (p. 25). This repetition serves to establish the crucifixion metaphor as thematically significant, rather than merely incidental, and prepares the reader to follow its development as the novel continues.

The implications of the metaphor expand to touch most of the ward's other patients a few chapters later, when Harding explains to McMurphy the procedures of electroshock therapy, the threat of which looms large in the life of each. "You are strapped to a table," he says, "shaped, ironically, like a cross, with a crown of electric sparks in place of thorns" (pp. 64–65). Chief Broom has experienced such therapy, and explains how, in his fog of withdrawal, he would travel in mind to

> the table shaped like a cross, with shadows of a thousand
> murdered men printed on it, silhouette wrists and ankles
> running under leather straps sweated green with use, a
> silhouette neck and head running up to a silver band goes
> across the forehead. (p. 117)

The epileptics alone are exempt from the threat of electric shock treatment, but only because they are spontaneously subject to shocks of their own, as we learn when Sefelt is discovered in an epileptic fit, "his hands . . . nailed out to each side with the palms up" just like men in the shock shop "strapped to the crossed table" (p. 154). Such use of the crucifixion image enables the novelist to render the microcosm that is the hospital as a world full of men experiencing, or threatened to experience, symbolic death by crucifixion in punishment for their inability to adjust to the patterns of life in the macrocosm without. As well as enduring the threat of physical crucifixion by electric shock, however, they must also sustain continuing spiritual crucifixion in the form of the psychoses that render them effectively dead and remove them from the sources of life.

Into this world of death, like "a giant come out of the sky" (p. 224), steps R. P. McMurphy, another who cannot conform, yet a man in sufficient possession of his faculties to stand aloof from the threat of death. Indeed, with his red hair, his loud voice, his boisterous humor, and his "man smell of dust and dirt from the open fields, and sweat, and work" (p. 91), he is the personification of life. All he need do is behave, and his release from the hospital is assured. But he is predestined not to do so, and from the moment of his entrance onto the ward until his selfless assault on Nurse Ratched, the novel is focused upon his developing recognition and acceptance of the inevitability and the necessity of his own crucifixion.

The conflict with Big Nurse that begins for McMurphy as a game becomes, through the process of this recognition, a self-chosen mission in which McMurphy attempts to effect the psychological salvation of his repressed fellows by sacrificing his own welfare. He comes, in the course of this recognition, to understand not only the nature of the force to which he is opposed, the emasculating pressure of a conformist society towards the repression of self in the interests of social concord, but also his own unique power within the microcosm in which he has been placed to operate as a redemptive counterforce, exemplifying a masculine drive towards the assertion of self. He emerges, at the novel's conclusion, as a type of Christ, giving his own life by choice for the salvation of others, and his experiences in the novel are presented in terms that repeatedly echo events in the life of Christ.

His way has been prepared, for example, by a voice in the wilderness, that of the former inmate Taber, who attempted in the past many of the reforms McMurphy undertakes in the present, and who preceded McMurphy as the first case of frontal lobotomy (symbolic and effective beheading) to be used as an example to the rest of the ward. He is surrounded by his apostles, as we learn in one of the novel's few pointedly brief paragraphs, where the Chief tells us he has been describing what happened "as McMurphy led the twelve of us toward the ocean" (p. 203). And though the trip to the ocean begins with Ellis impossibly pulling "his hands down off the nails in the wall" and telling Billy Bibbit to "be a fisher of men" (p. 198), it is in fact McMurphy who is the master fisher of men, and who teaches the others by example to be fishers of men themselves.

Whether in conceiving the fishing trip the author intended allusion to the early acrostic ICHTHUS, composed of the first letters of the Greek words for "Jesus Christ, Son of God, Savior," and in its Greek form the word for "fish" which caused fish to become Christ symbols in early Christian art, only the author himself could know. But that the fishing trip effects the establishment of a church to continue McMurphy's ministry is certain. It is on this trip, by spurring the men to an independence of action of which they have not been capable for years, that McMurphy initiates them into the McMurphy-like way of life.

He has by example been teaching them the principles of this life all along. By repeated assertions of his masculine individuality against the sterile conformity of life in the ward—by brushing his teeth at the wrong hour, by wearing his whale-emblem briefs in front of the Nurse, by singing loudly, by talking coarsely, by breaking windows, by throwing butter at the wall—he has consistently been demonstrating to them the possibility of self-assertion, and the helplessness of the establishment to resist it except by the most drastic measures. But it is on the fishing trip that he elicits at last their total commitment to the principles he has persistently exemplified. The trip is thus a modified mass baptism into the new religion of self-reliance (or self-assertion), and by its conclusion, McMurphy has largely prepared the disciples to carry on in his inevitable absence. As Chief Broom puts it, speaking as much for the others as for himself: "I was getting so's I could see some good in the life around me. McMurphy was teaching me" (p. 216).

The fishing trip offers as well the first unmistakable evidence that McMurphy has become a man of sorrows. He has been troubled since his arrival by the plight of his fellows, but only at this point is he approaching a full realization of his own identity as martyred redeemer. The Chief remarks that on the return to the hospital, "where the rest . . . looked red-cheeked and still full of excitement," McMurphy appeared "beat and worn out," and he goes on to say that he had "noticed McMurphy's exhaustion earlier, on the trip home" (p. 216). Shortly thereafter, we see McMurphy looking "dreadfully tired and strained and *frantic,* like there wasn't enough time left for something he had to do" (p. 218).

What McMurphy must do is complete the preparation of his disciples before he is overtaken by the fate he now sees as clearly unavoidable, and to which he yields with resignation. "Everybody could hear the helpless, cornered despair in McMurphy's voice," says Broom of the moment McMurphy stepped into the incident with the orderly Washington that triggered the chain of events leading to the end (p. 230). The helplessness results not from McMurphy's own lack of power to resist his fate, but from the awareness that renders him unwilling to ignore the otherwise irremediable need of his fellows. As the Chief, emerging from his own psychosis because of McMurphy, comes to focus with clarity on the issues involved, he begins to wonder how McMurphy could ever have slept, "plagued by a hundred faces like that, or two hundred, or a thousand" (p. 234). By the time McMurphy effects his disastrous assault on the Big Nurse, the Chief is completely aware that "it was our need that was making him push himself slowly up from sitting. . . . It was us that had been making him go on for weeks" (p. 267). His thoughts only echo the earlier words of Harding: "It is us . . . Us" (p. 258).

In his awareness, which makes him increasingly grow to resemble his teacher, the Chief, son of a tribe of Indian fishermen from Oregon (Peter was a fisherman), is clearly the rock upon which McMurphy establishes his church. Coming out of a shock treatment in full control of himself for the first time, the Chief is greeted by Harding in terms that had formerly applied to McMurphy alone, and realizes suddenly "how McMurphy must've felt all these months with these faces screaming up at him" (p. 243). And when McMurphy entertains transitory thoughts of escaping the ward, the Chief promises to stay on, because "somebody should stay here . . . to see that things don't start sliding back" (p. 257). Of course, McMurphy could not in fact have rejected his own role, and even if he had gone, says the Chief, he "would have *had* to come back. . . . It was like he'd signed on for the whole game and there wasn't any way of him breaking his contract" (p. 260).

Prior to completing his contract, however, McMurphy arranges the hilarious midnight party in the ward, clearly a grotesque version (but fully consistent with the values of the new religion) of the Last Supper, which is shared by the disciple who, in his fear the next day, will turn Judas, Billy Bibbit. The betrayal leads to Billy's suicide (Judas's end), which in its turn leads to McMurphy's attack on the Big Nurse (symbolically a rape), his frontal lobotomy, and his ultimate death. In death, he leaves behind not only the disciples, but also the Spirit, "McMurphy's presence still tromping up and down the halls" (p. 269), that disables the Nurse from ever regaining her old power over the ward.

The analogy between the lives of McMurphy and Christ is thus fairly complete, and the elements composing it are too numerous and too sustained—especially in their repetition—to be accidental or incidental. The analogy functions to elevate the action of the novel to a high plane of significance, for it suggests that contemporary civilization is suffering from a spiritual illness so severe, that a redirection of spiritual focus, such as that effected by the life and death of Christ, is in order. The analogy makes of the novel, moreover, a bible for contemporary action, because by systematically comparing McMurphy to Christ, it implies that the life of this contemporary redemptive figure must, like the life of Christ, offer a pattern for active emulation. The analogy culminates in the author's assignment of the narration to the particular "you" that the "giant come out of the sky" has most dramatically saved from the cuckoo's nest. In narrating the life of the martyred McMurphy, Chief Broom has become an apostle in the fullest sense of the word.

That the gospel Chief Broom prepares is intended for serious adoption by its readers is evidenced by Mr. Kesey's ensuing endeavor to emulate R. P. McMurphy's experiences in his own life. The failure of that endeavor, the dropping away of his own disciples and of the crowd of followers he initially collected, suggests that the doctrine he formulated in theory cannot be effected in practice. The cause of its practical failure is not hard to discover, for the religion he postulates, that of self-aggrandizement (call it by any contemporary term: "doing one's own thing," to the cost of the social fabric), fails to take into account original sin—the ineluctable depravity of man for which religion alone is necessary to atone.

It is no difficult task then, within the configurations of a purely fictional action, to demonstrate the felicitous effects of independent and self-centered activity. One is bound to sympathize with a fictional hero who performs as an adult the pranks we all engaged in as children but are inhibited from indulging in as adults ourselves. It is also safe to suppose that the people around such a hero, moved by a like sympathy with his basic human desire to indulge the self, will feel a natural inclination to act the way he does. But one is not bound to make a logical extension of fiction into fact, nor to suppose that such self-indulgence will have in reality the same meritorious outcome that it can be manipulated to achieve in art. One cannot gainsay the author's contention that the self-abnegation implicit in our conformity to social and ethical norms is dangerously frustrating. In theological, as well as psychological terms, it is inevitably frustrating to attempt to contain the beast within. Yet life presents little evidence that the release from frustration attained by allowing that beast a freer rein is to be more desired than feared.

It is ironic, of course, that Mr. Kesey should compare directly to Christ, the paradigm of humility, a man whose life is intended to exemplify the value of pride. Rather than lose the self in order to save it, the gospel according to Ken Kesey suggests, one must assert the self in order to save it. In contradiction to the fundamentally Christian view of human depravity, which considers the self one might assert as a potential Kurtz in the jungle, Mr. Kesey has predicated his novel upon the romantic philosophy that man is naturally benevolent, and that his natural actions, undistorted by the pressures of social necessity, will invariably conduce to the greatest good. Mr. Kesey fails at any point in his novel to consider the possibility that the natural, self-assertive actions of his protagonists might be at least as often destructive as the presumably unnatural actions of his antagonists— that all human action will in fact be subject to the same human limitations.

The problem in Mr. Kesey's philosophy is not that the Combine, his word for the establishment, is less evil than Mr. Kesey supposes (although it may possibly be so). It is rather that it is not the Combine which generates the evil Mr. Kesey observes, but the evil which generates the Combine, or at least makes of it what it is. The flaws in the system exist only because of anterior flaws in the men who created and maintain it. Attacking the system itself is attacking the symptom instead of the disease. That alternative systems will fall heir to the same human failings Mr. Kesey discovered. His Utopia collapsed as Utopias have persisted in doing.

But Mr. Kesey's Utopia was more foredoomed that most, since his prescription to combat the symptom, as we see in *One Flew Over the Cuckoo's Nest*, was simply a larger dose of the disease. The most fundamental precept of the religion Mr. Kesey exploits for his literary analogy is the danger of pride, the original sin in the sense of that self-love or self-absorption that makes all other sins possible. Yet the cardinal virtue in what might be termed the "cuckoo philosophy," repeatedly exemplified by McMurphy despite his paradoxical (and improbable) self-immolation, is that very self-loving self-assertion. Kesey suggests that by throwing butter at walls, breaking in windows, stealing boats, and doing in general whatever comes naturally, the inmates will become carefree and vital individuals at last. A Utopia composed of such self-centered children can spare itself the trouble of making any long-range plans.

Notes

1. Ken Kesey, *One Flew Over the Cuckoo's Nest* (New York: Signet, 1962), p. 20. Subsequent page references are included parenthetically within the text.

9
McMurphy and Yossarian as Politicians

◆◆◆◆◆◆◆◆◆◆◆◆◆◆

Jerome Klinkowitz

Randle Patrick McMurphy, the small-time gambler and brawler who seeks relief from prison work-farm drudgery by bluffing his way into a mental asylum, and Captain Yossarian, an Air Corps bombardier who thinks people (such as German gunners) are trying to kill him, are political forces within their own novels. McMurphy leads an open rebellion against the ward's authoritarian Head Nurse, and Yossarian debates conventional notions of authority, and even rational order, in war. Beyond their personal revolts, each argues for a new order of reality, whether it be in rejecting the plans for the mental and social hygiene an institutional state would impose, or speaking out against the routine absurdity that, through bureaucratic administration, can come to pass as fact.

Both McMurphy and Yossarian become politicians in a larger sense, as culture heroes for the bold new decade of the American 1960s. Their creators, Ken Kesey and Joseph Heller, wrote outside of the literary establishment, and neither pursued the usual course of a "developing" author. *One Flew Over the Cuckoo's Nest* and *Catch-22* are uniquely solitary works, far better-known than their authors, and each has served as a talisman to the new culture. Standing alone because they anticipated (rather than continued) a tradition, they became known as underground novels, popularized and propagated

Originally published in *The American 1960s: Imaginative Acts in a Decade of Change* (Ames: Iowa State University Press, 1980), pp. 20–32. Reprinted by permission.

by word-of-mouth recommendations quite independent of the establishment reviews and best-seller lists which continued to reflect the more closely drawn manners and morals (consider Saul Bellow, Bernard Malamud, John Updike) of the fifties. McMurphy and Yossarian were the first underground literary heroes of the new activist generation, proclaiming revolutionary new values which were as clear a signal as Kennedy's election that a new style and possibly a new reality were imminent.

One Flew Over the Cuckoo's Nest and *Catch-22* were first of all campus novels, and by the early 1960s academic conditions were such that a new market was available to insinuate these books into the consciousness of the youth culture, without using the traditional systems of distribution more likely to remain in conservative hands. The boom in higher education produced large classes of freshmen and sophomores, taught by a growing cadre of graduate assistants, and these books became two of the most widely taught novels in such circumstances. A decade earlier, English classes were just discovering the great modernist works of the 1920s; but as the sixties dawned, literature suddenly became a pressing contemporary concern. Kesey and Heller spoke directly to young collegians, in terms they soon would echo in their own protests against society. McMurphy and Yossarian were initially presented as heroes by a young, newly (and even prematurely) enfranchised group of teachers as the first chosen models in a new educational situation. Such coincidence and reinforcement between methods and materials is one of the many reasons why the sixties, as a decade of change, made such an immediate impact.

One Flew Over the Cuckoo's Nest speaks in the present tense, a signal of currency and of performance. The book *happens* like a movie. And it speaks directly to the reader, trusting the quality of *voice* to carry its effect far beyond the limited nature of its theme. "Who's the bull goose loony here?" shouts McMurphy as he bursts into the closely played world of the mental ward, its conformity and repression a perfect image of the fifties. What Mac says is important, but how he says it is what matters, embellishing his very presence with an aura of performance allusive to the wildness in America's past and the promise of her future:

> *"Then you tell Bull Goose Harding [the effeminate*

spokesman for the inmates] that R. P. McMurphy is
waiting to see him and that this hospital ain't big enough
for the two of us. I'm accustomed to being top man. I
been a bull goose catskinner for every gyppo logging
operation in the Northwest and bull goose gambler all the
way from Korea, was even a bull goose pea weeder on
that pea farm at Pendleton—so I figure if I'm bound to be
a loony, then I'm bound to be a stompdown dadgum one.
Tell this Harding that he either meets me man to man or
he's a yaller skunk and better be outta town by sunset."[1]

The inmates realize at once that he is a politician, even a mythic one, incorporating aspects of the car salesman, stock auctioneer, and sideshow pitchman. McMurphy hits the ward like a bolt of summer lightning, not just for what he is in himself, but for what needs to be done in the hospital.

The hospital Mac has faked his way into is like none other in American fact or fiction. Phone wires whistle in the walls, electric current roars through conduits to appliances, fog machines deliberately obscure the grounds, and nuts-and-bolts technicians pull spare parts in and out of the patients at will. These images are metaphorical, at least to the reader. But to the novel's narrator, a Columbia River Indian named "Chief Broom" Bromden, they are strikingly real. Although officially described as a mental case, the Chief in fact suffers from (or enjoys the benefit of) a rich visual imagination. What may only be subtle intention on the part of the Head Nurse becomes in Bromden's mind a startling, physical actuality, and her manner of ward discipline is not only expressed by him in fantastic mechanical terms, but is extended to a larger vision of society, entirely restructured according to the Nurse's ideal of absolute, repressive order.

Chief Bromden's mind resists the Nurse's plan, and by playing deaf and dumb he is able to overhear what the other inmates miss. What the fifties called a disability, the sixties would redefine as great and touching eloquence. But his imagination has an even more important role in this novel. It is the fertile field on which McMurphy's ideas fall, the sensitive screen against which his flamboyant actions are played. If the Chief has expressed the imaginative truth of the Nurse's repressive manner, he is also the one to mythologize McMurphy's resistance and rebellion. A hero such as Mac needs first of all to be perceived as a hero; and as our eyes and ears in this novel, the conventionally mute Chief Bromden becomes the expression of McMurphy's greatness.

A limited and closely defined set of images fills Chief Bromden's mind: the action among the ward's inmates, the Big Nurse's regimentation and more subtle manipulation of those inmates, the foreboding institutional and technological atmosphere (described as "operations of the Combine"), and McMurphy's posture in opposition to it all. Mac is more vitally healthy than the pallid, insipid patients, for his own life of self-assertion is in direct contrast to the passive, depressive, and victimized stance inmates like Harding and Bibbit have taken toward the world. Because he has led the footloose life of a drifter, Mac has remained untouched by the Combine, which would use marriage and responsibility as pressures molding potential individuals into suburban ciphers, one interchangeable with another. *One Flew Over the Cuckoo's Nest* was one of the first novels to deal imaginatively with the hidden persuaders, the organization men, the lonely crowd, and other current sociological images of the fifties that characterized a world of plenty the sixties generation would not worship but fear. Very shortly the age of affluence would be condemned as spiritually impoverished. The popularity of Chief Bromden's fears about the Combine is among the first signs of a change in cultural sentiment:

> *The ward is a factory for the Combine. It's for fixing up mistakes made in the neighborhoods and in the schools and in the churches, the hospital is. When a completed product goes back out into society, all fixed up as good as new,* **better** *than new sometimes, it brings joy to the Big Nurse's heart; something that came in all twisted different is now a functioning, adjusted component, a credit to the whole outfit and a marvel to behold. Watch him sliding across the land with a welded grin, fitting into some nice little neighborhood where they're just now digging trenches along the street to lay pipes for city water. He's happy with it. He's adjusted to surroundings finally. . . . (p. 38)*

In the 1950s social conformity had been the ideal for material progress, and in the forties it was an even loftier virtue as part of the war effort.

The new culture in the sixties questioned both, and Kesey emphasizes the fatal nature of the "Combine" by making its principal victim the Vanishing American who narrates this novel, a man who is being psychically destroyed by the same forces of social progress that killed his tribe.

Against these social forces, which by the 1960s had come to be perceived as threats, McMurphy places himself as a revolutionary hero. He is first of all a disruptionist, against the Big Nurse in particular and authority in general, and especially against the type of authority that inhibits self-expression and places limits on the individual. Like disruptionists of the coming decade, he sees that most of his acts must be theatrical, and much of his early effort is spent in gaming and baiting the Big Nurse. He challenges votes at her group meetings, smears her nurses' station window, disrupts her ward routine—all staged to the pleasure of the observing inmates. Even the pettiest acts are deliberately symbolic. They weaken the Nurse, but more importantly they strengthen the men. Randle Patrick McMurphy is the first fictional hero to practice that key strategy of sixties leadership: *raising the consciousness of the people.* The ward inmates represent a cross section of American society, but his most responsive pupil is Chief Broom, a Native American, the First American, whom the progress of events has reduced to a deathlike silence. McMurphy restores the Chief to life, "blows him up whole again," and so reanimates America—just what the culturally regenerative movements of the sixties sought to do.

McMurphy's role as animator is worth looking at more closely. Although the ward he checks into is physically and emotionally lifeless, its spirit broken by the strictures of the Big Nurse, McMurphy does not try to change any of its essential characteristics. Rather, he transforms it into something positive. He does not deny that he and the others are "loonies," but rather asserts his looniness as part of the mechanics of greatness (he will become "bull goose loony") and offers the same potential to anyone else. "Mad is beautiful," McMurphy preaches to these self-defeated patients who have let society's label destroy them. The therapies Mac develops do not contradict the inmates' condition but rather exploit their so-called disabilities in order to create a new source of strength. One of the happiest moments in the ward (and one of the most enjoyably readable sections of the novel) is an interlude when the whole crew plays Monopoly, replete with bizarre rules and hallucinated playing pieces conceivable only in a madhouse. The equally improbable fishing trip lets every man play his own role to the fullest. McMurphy is truly a transformative hero. He changes the terms under which they are living, rather than changing their lives themselves. Laughter is his great weapon: "that big wide-open laugh of his. Dials twitch in the control panel at the sound of it" (p. 17). It is the one thing an otherwise totally helpless person can do, McMurphy teaches the men. And Chief Bromden remembers it as a weapon his father and other tribesmen used against the government. Though laughter is a physical expression, its substance is intellectual, even imaginative. In this way McMurphy is advocating a proletarian revolution of the mind; it is his new valuation of the terms of life that makes him a threat to the establishment. McMurphy is inventing a new way of perceiving reality, which is nothing less than a new reality itself.

The radical nature of McMurphy's challenge to the establishment is shown by the way the establishment strikes back. Emotional castration has kept the lesser inmates in line, but Mac's challenge has come from his imagination, and so castration of his mind—lobotomy—is the Nurse's ultimate response. "I guess if she can't cut below the belt she'll do it above the eyes" (p. 180), Mac tells the Chief. For his part, Mac stays with the group and sacrifices himself for it—a new style of American heroism. The heroic tradition had been for a Natty Bumppo to strike off on his own, or for a Captain Ahab to sacrifice the group for his own ideal. "Anointest my head with conductant," Mac tells the electroshock therapist who begins his crucifixion, "Do I get a crown of thorns?" (p. 270). The Chief remarks several times how McMurphy has been weakened by his quest. As the men increase, Mac decreases, until by the end, when the inmates have taken control of their lives and the Chief has performed his superhuman act of throwing a hydrotherapy fount through the window and taking off for freedom, he is completely effaced from the novel. But only in body. The men walk with his swagger, boast with his bravado. McMurphy was the restorative spirit, and they have been restored.

One Flew Over the Cuckoo's Nest presents a transformed vision of reality as well. And not just because the book's narrator has a richly imaginative way of perceiving things. Rather, that narrator has the special ability to play with the technical givens of his situation. He doesn't suffer from the mechanization of the Big Nurse's world; instead, he incorporates all its facets as elements of imaginative play, in a game he—not the Nurse—controls. Even routine exposition benefits from this trick, making a richer, more imaginative, and ironically more personalized world to live in. "A tall bony old guy, dangling from a wire screwed in between his shoulder blades, met McMurphy and me at the door when the aides brought us in," the Chief narrates. "He looked us over with yellow, scaled eyes and shook his head. 'I wash my hands of the whole deal,' he told one of the colored aides, and the wire drug him off down the hall" (p. 264). The first characterization of the Big Nurse herself has been similarly composed of such native elements as the Chief finds handy for the art he can make from his world:

> *She slides through the door with a gust of cold and locks*
> *the door behind her and I see her fingers trail across the*
> *polished steel—tip of each finger the same color as her*
> *lips. Funny orange. Like the tip of a soldering iron.*
> *(pp. 3–4)*

Throughout the novel Chief Bromden plays with his made-up images, his junk-sculpture from the manic-depressive ward. The Nurse leaves a lipstick stain on a coffee cup, but the Chief believes "that color on the rim of the cup must be from heat, touch of her lips set it smoldering" (p. 149). The importance of the Chief's technique is obvious when we see the other typical activity of his mind: reconstructing idyllic memories of his young manhood on the Columbia River, before the government dispossessed his tribe. Both procedures are vital to his psychic health, as he refreshes himself in happy memories and actively works on the present to create a life of fiction. As the sixties developed, thinkers as various as psychiatrist R. D. Laing and philosopher Norman O. Brown would propose the same therapy to the culture at large.

But foremost is the way McMurphy, and especially the idea of McMurphy, operates on Chief Bromden's mind. Mac fills the Indian's imagination as the hero needed to revive him:

> *The iron in his boot heels crackled lightning out of the*
> *tile. He was the logger again, the swaggering gambler,*
> *the big redheaded Irishman, the cowboy out of the TV set*

walking down the middle of the street to meet a dare.
(p. 189)

As he has played with the mechanical image of the Nurse, Chief Bromden embellishes the person of Randle McMurphy until it represents nearly every hero America has known for her mythic sustenance. For what he must do, McMurphy is made larger than life, too large even to be believable, just as the Chief's narration is too poetic to pass for day-to-day speech. "I been silent so long now," he tells us, "it's gonna roar out of me like floodwaters and you think the guy telling this is ranting and raving my *God;* you think this is too horrible to have really happened, this is too awful to be the truth!" (p. 8). Cultural conditions at the turn of the sixties demanded a prophet. "It's still hard for me to have a clear mind thinking on it," the Chief admits. "But it's the truth even if it didn't happen" (p. 8).

Kesey's novel invents a new reality by means of voice, especially voice expressing an imaginatively new construction of the world. Joseph Heller's *Catch-22* reaches deeper for its reconstruction. Although the novel does have a surface action, with characters and themes drawn from World War II, its real substance is language, especially the grammar and syntax which philosophers tell us intimate the deep structure of reality. Such criticism began in America with Noam Chomsky's studies of transformational grammar in 1957, and structuralism as a method became popular here only in the 1960s. But even for subject matter, one can't forget that Heller's picture of World War II eclipses conventional realism. For one, it comes nearly two decades after the event, after the country had been through Korea and was gearing up for Vietnam. In 1961, hardly anybody was writing realistic fiction about World War II, and the author of *Catch-22* was not about to begin.

Instead, Heller's purpose was larger: he was redefining World War II as a way of revising our notions of what passes for reality. And at the very first came a new grammar to reflect this orientation. "The Texan turned out to be good-natured, generous and likeable," we are told early on. "In three days nobody could stand him."[2] Everything that comes up for discussion is handled in this fractured rhetoric. "Colonel Cargill, General Peckem's troubleshooter, was a forceful, ruddy man," we are told.

Before the war he had been an alert, hard-hitting,

> *aggressive marketing executive. He was a very bad*
> *marketing executive. Colonel Cargill was so awful a*
> *marketing executive that his services were much sought*
> *after by firms eager to establish losses for tax purposes.*
> *(p. 27)*

Heller continues at paragraph length with such descriptions, and it turns out there are very real (if financially innovative) reasons for Cargill's success. But they are expressed in a total butchery of conventional syntax and reason: "He had to start at the top and work his way down" (p. 27); "He was a self-made man who owed his lack of success to nobody," and so on. Heller is not only inventing a new way to perceive reality; he is inventing a new reality, based on a reversal of values carried over from the earlier world view. The big surprise is that most everyone assumed that earlier world view still prevailed.

The military provides a perfect setting for the logical proof of such an illogical re-creation of reality, and is an example accessible to most Americans. Being in the Army, or just watching it operate, gives one the impression that this is a colossal ship of fools, an absurdist enterprise made operational only by its vaguely assumed importance of mission. *Catch-22* makes fun of Army bureaucracy, Army logic, and Army inefficiency. But it also makes a deeper impression than the many popular entertainments of the time, such as Mac Hyman's *No Time for Sergeants*, Phil Silvers' *Sergeant Bilko/You'll Never Get Rich* television series, and their imitators. Like Kesey, Joseph Heller enjoys playing with the imaginative possibilities of off-kilter situations, and his virtuosity with language creates an enjoyable, verbally artistic picture:

> *The colonel dwelt in a vortex of specialists who were*
> *still specializing in trying to determine what was*
> *troubling him. They hurled lights into his eyes to see if*
> *he could see, rammed needles into nerves to hear if he*
> *could feel. There was a urologist for his urine, a*
> *lymphologist for his lymph, an endocrinologist for his*
> *endocrines, a psychologist for his psyche, a dermatologist*
> *for his derma; there was a pathologist for his pathos, a*
> *cystologist for his cysts, and a bald and pedantic*
> *cetologist from the zoology department at Harvard who*

> *had been shanghaied ruthlessly into the Medical Corps by*
> *a faulty anode in an I.B.M. machine and spent his*
> *sessions with the dying colonel trying to discuss* Moby-
> Dick *with him. (p. 15)*

From the silliness of "isms" and "ists," which pervades modern life far beyond the Army, Heller has extended and embellished the situation, from the reasonableness of "urologist/urine" to the craziness of "pathologist/pathos." The root of his method is the faulty syllogism, the unequal equation that urologist is to urine as pathologist is to pathos, but such wacky structures are revealed as the principles on which a new reality has been built. If a Harvard cetologist can get drafted into the Medical Corps, how less ridiculous is it for him to discuss Melville with his patients? In this way Heller's novel defines and clarifies a new reality we might not otherwise believe was there.

Needless to say, American novels did not provide such phenomenological service in the 1950s. But neither does Heller go the way of the French *nouveau roman*, for he animates *Catch-22* with the behavior of living human beings whose deep and interesting personalities must respond to the phenomenological surface so described. Yossarian is the foremost example. He is the one combatant who suffers from the otherwise paranoid fears, that "they are trying to kill me," which only the transformed reality of World War II makes real. Because of his ultimate reasonability in the face of compounded absurdity, Yossarian is the one to challenge the orders which systematically increase the number of combat missions to be flown before the men can complete them. But his personal life shows that he is, just as much as anyone, involved in the new reality. He participates in it, as parody, by censoring letters with a bored irrationality equal to anything his commanders might force upon him. To break the monotony, he invents syntactic games. One day he censors all modifiers, the next, adverbs.

> *The next day he made war on articles. He reached a much*
> *higher plane of creativity the following day when he*
> *blacked out everything in the letters but* a, an *and* the.
> *That erected more dynamic intralinear tensions, he felt,*
> *and in just about every case left a message far more*
> *universal. (p. 8)*

120

He signs his name "Washington Irving," later "Irving Washington," planting the seeds for a CID investigation only a bit less Byzantine than the novel's action itself.

Yossarian plays with sentences, but Heller uses *Catch-22* to show that our own sentences have placed us in structures we cannot fulfill, such as Colonel Cathcart's hopeless situation, completely self-created and expressed to himself in terms of a grammatical ideal: "He could measure his own progress only in relation to others, and his idea of excellence was to do something at least as well as all the men his own age who were doing the same thing even better" (p. 185). Other roles are fulfilled all too well. Milo Minderbinder develops a trading syndicate equal to any of the large corporations which asserted their supremacy after World War II, and his method is located in the same bizarre language structures:

> *I make a profit of three and a quarter cents an egg by*
> *selling them for four and a quarter cents an egg to the*
> *people in Malta I buy them from for seven cents an egg.*
> *Of course, I don't make the profit. The syndicate makes*
> *the profit. And everybody has a share. (p. 226)*

His M & M Enterprises stands simply for Milo Minderbinder, with the "&" added "to nullify the impression that the syndicate was a one-man operation" (p. 248). Milo can no more eliminate the middleman in his operation (himself) than the nurses can eliminate the middleman in the case of the head-to-toe bandaged soldier in white, where each morning a bottle of intravenous fluid is plugged in and a bottle of urine taken away. To eliminate the middleman would be to eliminate the soldier himself. Like the "&" in Milo's enterprises, he is the necessary grammatical structure needed to make this mad world work. To show the totally arbitrary nature of war, Milo contracts bomb runs for the Germans, taking on bridges, emplacements, and finally his own airfield. For tactical warfare, at least, the middleman has been eliminated.

Yossarian is a restorative hero because he wants to wake up those around him to the hideous facts the Army's new reality is obscuring:

> *"They're trying to kill me," Yossarian told him*
> *calmly.*
> *"No one's trying to kill you," Clevinger cried.*

> *"Then why are they shooting at me?" Yossarian asked.*
> *"They're shooting at* everyone," *Clevinger answered.*
> *"They're trying to kill everyone."*
> *"And what difference does that make?" (p. 16)*

He is an expert at fending off the Army's perverse logic. He refuses to fly more missions. When the Colonel asks him what would happen if everyone acted that way, Yossarian replies that then he'd be an even greater fool to act differently.

Yossarian discovers a deeper reality beneath the Army's new provisions. The Colonel's self-aggrandizement and Milo's mania for capitalism convince him that there is a more substantial goal than bombing Germans. The way, in fact, is a game board on which senior officers battle to seize each other's power, and the real progress of the war is the advancement of their own careers. General Peckem of Special Services develops a master plan to incorporate all of the Air Corps units into his own, only to be subverted by Colonel Scheisskopf, whose solitary aim is to assemble more and more men to march for him. Some tactics developed in World War II work much better against the other generals than against the Germans. In Heller's own time, a war was being fought in Vietnam which yielded none of the traditional military goals, but which amply satisfied militaristic needs: a corps of senior officers, stalled in rank by the vicissitudes of a peacetime Army, were given the combat commands they needed for proper career advancement. Major Josiah Bunting's novel *The Lionheads* (1972) drew the same conclusion from actual Vietnam command experience, but Heller's *Catch-22* sensed these conditions in American culture in 1961, just as the Vietnam War began.

The repetitious, cumulative structure of *Catch-22* reflects the non-linear form of Heller's new reality. Nothing develops in clear succession, nothing advances in a clear line. Rather, scenes are repeated over and over again, each time coming into sharper focus, until at the end the reader is overwhelmed by an event, anticipated several times in *déjà vu* so that all its elements carry twice or even ten times the strength they might normally have. The death of Snowden is the clearest case. Its cumulative repetition controls the mood of the whole novel, which gradually shifts from hilarity to horror. Time and space are reconstituted as elements of reality, simply because they are experienced differently in the world of *Catch-22*.

Aspects of military bureaucracy also contribute to a reshaped nature of the real. The "dead soldier in Yossarian's tent" is a problem because he took off on a mission, and died on it, before the duty officer could check him in. Since the command does not officially know that he "lived," it cannot report his death. When Hungry Joe's light plane crashes into a mountainside, Doc Daneeka is declared dead, a victim of the opposite situation: he had added his name to the flight manifest as an easy way to earn flight pay. Yossarian receives a medal for fouling a bomb run, since the Colonel can think of no other way to cover the embarrassment. And so on, to the point of debasing all values of life and death, courage and cowardice, heroics and dishonor.

To be effective, America must fashion a new definition of heroism. This was the conclusion social philosophers and even natural scientists came to as the decade ended. The Promethean hero who provided a model to expand and develop the country was no longer adequate to a world of depleted resources and diminished environment. Notions of success and failure had to be readjusted; the new hero became Protean, as described by Joseph Meeker (*The Comedy of Survival*, 1974), Paul Shepard (*The Tender Carnivore and the Sacred Game*, 1973), Loree Rackstraw (*Earth Mother and Father Time*, in progress), and others. Curiously, Heller was able to find an image for this new heroism within World War II. "You put too much stock in *winning wars*," the old Italian man tells Nately. He explains that "the real trick lies in *losing* wars, in knowing which wars can be *lost*. Italy has been losing wars for centuries, and just see how splendidly we've done nonetheless." France wins and languishes; Germany loses and prospers. "Italy won a war in Ethiopia and promptly stumbled into serious trouble. Victory gave us such insane delusions of grandeur"—the Prometheus complex, Rackstraw and her colleagues would later suggest—"that we helped start a world war we hadn't a chance of winning. But now that we are losing again, everything has taken a turn for the better, and we will certainly come out on top again if we succeed in being defeated" (p. 240).

The old man's logic takes the same form as all *Catch-22* rhetoric. Its strategy of systematic reversal underscores the point that a new reality, quite the opposite of the old, has taken hold; the screwed-up action of the Army only represents an undirected foundering among these new currents. Heller's point has not been just to mimic and ridicule the chaos encountered with the coming of such a new world, but rather to clarify the changes in values so that life may be lived with more happiness and success. "Anything worth living for is worth dying for," Nately argues. But the old Italian corrects him and puts him back on course. "And anything worth dying for," he tells the young soldier, "is certainly worth living for" (p. 242).

Although it never appeared on a best-seller list, *Catch-22* became an underground classic in the 1960s, selling over six million copies, more than twice the cumulative sales of the top listed novel of 1961, *The Agony and the Ecstasy.* The only serious novel to outsell it, in fact, has been *One Flew Over the Cuckoo's Nest*, according to figures published in *The Wilson Quarterly* (Winter 1978). To find better-selling fiction, one must go to the pulp masterpieces of Jacqueline Susann, Erich Segal, and Richard Bach. And even there the margin above *Catch-22* is less than fifteen percent.

In a country as commercialized as the United States, it is difficult to identify authentic popular culture within the products of mass-media entertainment, and even harder to single out legitimate cultural trends. For novels, one way is to see if phrases and attitudes work their way out of the books and into the popular ambience of the times. Kesey's novel does this in reverse: it builds itself out of elements widely available (and operative) in the popular culture, from the multiform images of McMurphy to the mythic stature of its narrator, the Indian, Chief Bromden. But *Catch-22* was a more formative novel. Ostensibly about World War II, it described that conflict in terms that were to become innovatively accurate for a war just beginning in Vietnam, a war that defined all previous stereotypes and that could be discussed coherently only in the wacky new grammar Heller's novel had invented. "Catch-22" became a code word for any self-contradicting bureaucratic order in society, used by people who never read the novel. And the qualities of Yossarian became a new heroic image for the decade, a new image for the male star, whether for Dustin Hoffman playing in *The Graduate*, Robert Blake in *Electra-Glide in Blue*, or Alan Arkin playing Yossarian himself in Mike Nichol's film of *Catch-22*.

That movie audiences did not see adaptations of *One Flew Over the Cuckoo's Nest* and *Catch-22* until after the decade ended is even better proof that, as novels, they existed outside the pressure of commercial entertainment. If a book is successful as an economic investment, the film version usually comes a year later. Advertising, paperback publication, and film distribution reinforce each other in "tie-ins," and the product is marketed like an LP record—or, better yet, like a line of frozen pizzas. Under such conditions, it is hard to tell whether the American public is responding to a deeply felt image in its developing culture, or whether it is being sold a bill of goods.

The movies made from Kesey's and Heller's novels came much later, in the early 1970s. In their case a complementary principle of the American film industry was employed: if some films are made in response to commercial success, others try to manufacture a commercial success out of something already existing in the popular culture. Here the people supply the product to the industry, instead of the other way around. For nearly ten years, McMurphy and Yossarian had helped express the redirection of a culture. They were popular far beyond the already large sales of their novels; their attitudes and beliefs pervaded American life, so that by the later 1960s they marched in the streets to protest similar institutional and bureaucratic monstrosities perpetrated by some who commanded our government. Davy Crockett, Daniel Boone, Paul Bunyan, and other such representative American characters were not created by a commercial entertainment complex, but their authentic popularity made them apt materials for commercial use. McMurphy and Yossarian described the new reality underlying the politics of the 1960s, and the extent of their popularity, in their respective novels and films, flanks that decade almost as neatly as the numerological way we count off decades themselves.

Notes

1. Ken Kesey, *One Flew Over the Cuckoo's Nest* (New York: Viking, 1962), p. 19. All subsequent references are to this edition and are parenthesized in the text.

2. Joseph Heller, *Catch-22* (New York: Simon & Schuster, 1961), p. 9. All subsequent references are to this edition and are parenthesized in the text.

10
Kesey and Vonnegut: Preachers of Redemption

●●●●●●●●●●●●●●

James R. Tunnell

Apathetic is a word frequently used to describe today's society. Webster defines *apathetic* as "void of feeling," "unemotional" or "indifferent." Actually, the sin of indifference and unconcern has plagued mankind in every age. The medieval church called it by its Latin name, *acedia*, and listed it as one of the seven deadly sins. Through the centuries *acedia* has been variously translated as "laziness" or "indolence," "boredom" or "depression." But although it is as old as the human race, apathy uniquely characterizes Western society in this twentieth century.

Much of the literature of our time mirrors the results of the sin of *acedia*: estrangement, meaninglessness, dereliction, melancholia. Consider, for example, the tales of Kafka, the novels of Faulkner and Camus, the plays of Sartre, Albee or Tennessee Williams. Indeed— borrowing the title of Nathan A. Scott, Jr.'s book on theology and modern literature—one might say that many of today's writings are "rehearsals of discomposure."

In the past decade, however, a significant new group of writers has emerged on the American scene. They are, all of them, skillful

Originally published in *The Christian Century* (11 November 1972), pp. 1180–83. Reprinted by permission. Copyright 1972, Christian Century Foundation, Chicago, IL 60605.

practitioners of their craft, forceful and imaginative; but their primary significance lies in their new affirmation of personhood. They preach to our time a new kind of redemption: a redemption from the deadly sin of *acedia*. Among this array of writers, the two who attack the problem of apathy most explicitly and argue most persuasively for individual dignity are Ken Kesey and Kurt Vonnegut, Jr., in their respective novels *One Flew Over the Cuckoo's Nest* and *Slaughterhouse-Five*.

Kesey's *One Flew Over the Cuckoo's Nest* is set in a state mental hospital. The hero and, apparently, the only sane person in the whole novel is one Randle McMurphy, a brawling, lusty, fun-loving Irishman. Tired of hoeing peas at a prison farm, McMurphy feigns insanity for a chance at the softer life of the mental hospital. But he gets more than he bargains for. Once committed, he is placed in a ward dominated by "Big Nurse," a sadistic tyrant whose aim is to run her ward "like a smooth, accurate, precision-made machine."[1] McMurphy, convinced that the policies of Big Nurse are petty and demeaning, defies her. As the story unfolds, it becomes plain that McMurphy symbolizes individuality, courage and humanity, whereas Big Nurse symbolizes bigness, conformity and inhumanity.

McMurphy's conflict with Big Nurse begins in fun. Quickly sizing up things on the day of his arrival, he wagers with his fellow patients, who live in mortal fear of her, that he will be able to rattle Big Nurse and throw a kink into her routine before the week is out. And he does. His first morning on the ward, clothed only in a hunting cap and a pair of black satin undershorts emblazoned with white whales, he walks out of the men's room to confront Big Nurse about not having received his green hospital uniform. After that first encounter, hardly a day passes without Big Nurse getting her comeuppance from McMurphy.

The turning point in the story comes when McMurphy, after several weeks of hospitalization, discovers to his amazement that most of the patients on the ward are there by their own consent. He himself, being a ward of the state, had no choice about his commitment or the duration of his confinement. But he cannot believe that free human beings would voluntarily submit to such dehumanizing treatment. At this point a conflict that began in jest becomes utterly serious. McMurphy's struggle with Big Nurse takes on the character of a life mission. By precept and example, he sets out to cure his fellow patients of their sickness of will.

The cards, of course, are stacked against him. McMurphy's assertion of his own individuality is taken as evidence of his insanity. The more he asserts his personhood, the more Big Nurse becomes determined to "cure" him of his rebellious idiosyncrasies and his uncooperative behavior. He is subjected to mind-changing shock treatments. But these, as McMurphy says, only "charge my battery" (p. 276). When all else fails, Big Nurse convinces the resident physicians that surgery is the only answer. So a lobotomy is performed, and McMurphy is left a helpless vegetable.

In describing McMurphy's anguish, Kesey employs some obvious Christ symbols. The shock treatments are administered on a table "shaped like a cross" (p. 126). When told before his first shock treatment that the graphite salve smeared on his temples is a conductant, McMurphy replies: "Anointest my head with conductant. Do I get a crown of thorns?" (p. 270). Clearly, Kesey intends McMurphy to be a twentieth-century suffering and redemptive servant.

What is most important, however, is the transformation that occurs in the lives of the patients as the result of McMurphy's "passion." When McMurphy first arrived, the other patients in the ward, apathetic, cowed and docile, had long ago given up the struggle to assert themselves against Big Nurse's authority. One of the patients explains their self-understanding by saying:

> All of us here are rabbits of varying ages and degrees,
> hippity-hopping through our Walt Disney world. Oh,
> don't misunderstand me, we're not in here because we
> are rabbits—we'd be rabbits wherever we were—we're all
> in here because we can't adjust to our rabbithood. We
> need a good strong wolf like the nurse to teach us our
> place. (p. 62)

Angered by such nonsense, McMurphy insists that men are men. And he sets about showing his wardmates a lifestyle that reflects the joy and the freedom of authentic humanity. On their part the patients, having experienced real humanity through McMurphy, are less and less willing to conform to a dehumanizing system. Courage, they discover, can be as contagious as fear.

After the impact of McMurphy, Big Nurse is never able to re-establish her tyrannical order. Even after he has been silenced, McMurphy continues to permeate the hospital. One patient, in words reminiscent of the Gospels, remarks that McMurphy's presence is still felt, "tramping up and down the halls and laughing out loud in the meetings and singing in the latrines" (p. 307). At the end of the novel, Big Nurse's ward is being dismantled patient by patient. Some ask to be transferred to other wards, but most of them go "flying east and west, away from the cuckoo's nest" to new lives and new futures.

Rabbits are said not only to be timid and docile but also to have short memories—that is how nature protects them from going mad under the constant threat of being killed. But man's short memory regarding the atrocities he has repeatedly committed against his kind is no dispensation of nature; it is rather a refusal, more or less willed, to call to mind his own frightfulness. This is the theme of *Slaughterhouse Five*, the unusual war novel by Kurt Vonnegut, Jr.

The story focuses on a pathetic character named Billy Pilgrim. It has no real heroes because, as Vonnegut explains, most of the characters are arbitrary victims of chance. Billy (like Vonnegut himself) was drafted during World War II, taken captive during the Battle of the Bulge, and imprisoned in an underground slaughterhouse in the German city of Dresden. From his bunker, Billy (again like Vonnegut) witnessed the fire-bombing of Dresden carried out by American and British planes in February 1945—a raid in which 135,000 people were killed.

The destruction of Dresden is the event around which the story revolves. In an introductory chapter, Vonnegut compares his obsession with this single event to the experience of Lot's wife, who, looking back at the fiery destruction of Sodom and Gomorrah, was turned into a pillar of salt. This is Vonnegut's way of acknowledging, tongue in cheek, that his novel is bound to be a failure since it is written by a pillar of salt.

Death appears in some form on almost each page of this story. Sometimes it is the death of persons close to Billy—his father or his wife—sometimes of people he does not know at all; and sometimes it is one death, sometimes the death of hundreds or thousands. Vonnegut punctuates each mention of death with the phrase, "So it goes." The inanity of this endlessly repeated refrain suggests how apathetic, indifferent, and insensitive people have become in the face of death.

The fact is that the fire-bombing of Dresden was the most disastrous single raid of World War II: the number of civilians killed in it was twice that killed in the atom-bombing of Hiroshima. Moreover, it seems to have been an exercise in sheer terror. Vonnegut quotes a military historian's statement that Dresden was not a strategic city and that the raid served no essential military purpose. But the most important thing about this raid is that it has largely been forgotten. Vonnegut seems to be saying that the memory of Dresden ought to be kept alive so as to serve as a deterrent against repetition of such horrors. People may respond, rabbit fashion, that the only possible way to deal with such horrors is to become numb to them. But numbness to horror, the story reveals, dehumanizes us.

Billy Pilgrim is an ironic illustration of this theme. He is a person who has become "unstuck in time." Vonnegut describes Billy's life as a kind of spinning roulette wheel on which past, present, and future events are indistinguishable from each other. Billy even boards a flying saucer and visits a planet in outer space whose citizens share with him their cosmic secrets. The most important of these secrets is that time must be seen in its wholeness—taken in, like a mountain range, at a single glance. Yet, having been allowed a glimpse of this "cosmic secret," he is unwilling and unable to assimilate its implications for his own life. And herein is the tragedy of Billy Pilgrim.

Many times over, Billy experiences in memory the bombing of Dresden and the other horrors of war. Yet that memory does nothing to shape his life nor to make him more sensitive and compassionate. After his ignominious military career, he marries the right girl and becomes a wealthy optometrist. He drives a Cadillac, espouses right-wing causes, and does quite well according to the standards of the society in which he lives. Presently he fathers a son who is an alcoholic failure in high school but a success as a Green Beret in Vietnam. Like so many people around him, Billy tries "to construct a life that [makes] sense from things found in gift shops."[2] But his life does not make sense: he ends up rich but bored and unhappy.

Yet, strangely, redeeming grace invades Billy's existence. He reads *The Gospel from Outer Space*, a book by his favorite science fiction writer, Kilgore Trout, who presents his own version of the story of Jesus. Trout tells how a visitor from outer space, coming to earth to learn why Christians find it so easy to be cruel, discovers that the trouble started with slipshod storytelling on the part of the early Christians. The purpose of the New Testament writers was to teach people to be merciful and kind even to their most despised neighbors. But at the hands of their careless heirs the original message became warped. "'Before you kill somebody, make sure he isn't well connected. . . .' And that thought had a brother: 'There are right people to lynch.' Who? People not well connected . . .'" (p. 94). So the visitor from outer space gives the earth a new gospel:

> In it, Jesus really was a nobody, and a pain in the neck to a lot of people with better connections than he had. He still got to say all the lovely and puzzling things he said in the other Gospels.
>
> So the people amused themselves one day by nailing him to a cross in the ground. There couldn't possibly be any repercussions, the lynchers thought. The reader would have to think that, too, since the new Gospel hammered home again and again what a nobody Jesus was.
>
> And then, just before the nobody died, the heavens opened up, and there was thunder and lightning. The voice of God came crashing down. He told the people that he was adopting the bum as his son, giving him the full powers and privileges of The Son of the Creator of the Universe throughout all eternity. God said this: From this moment on, He will punish horribly anybody who torments a bum who has no connections!
> (pp. 94–95)

Kesey and Vonnegut occupy different pulpits, but both speak to the same congregation and proclaim similar messages of redemption. The two novelists are addressing themselves to those who, amid the conformity and barrenness of our time, are searching for some vestige of personal integrity and some measure of human kindness.

For Kesey the key word is *courage*. The theologian Harvey Cox argues that modern man's "most debilitating proclivity is *not* his pride. . . . it is his sloth, his unwillingness to be everything man was intended to be." In our kind of world it takes courage to think one's own thoughts and make one's own decisions, to feel for and with others, and to laugh at times. Yet these things are the essential ingredients in the human personality. Kesey grants that a cross may be the price of personal integrity, but he also proclaims that crosses can be redemptive and that resurrection is always the final word.

For Vonnegut the key word is *compassion*. The psychotherapist Rollo May insists that the opposite of love is not hate but apathy. Love means passion and feeling, and apathy is the withdrawal of feeling. To be apathetic is to choose not to be involved; or, in May's words, it is a "gradual letting go of involvement until one finds that life itself has gone by." Vonnegut's plea is: "Don't let yourself adjust to the unthinkable and the unbearable. There's enough inhumanity in the world without adding to it. Be kind. Open up. Reach out. Have a heart."

Kesey and Vonnegut would never be classified as "religious writers." Yet each of them in his own way has made an important contribution to a contemporary understanding of Christian redemption.

Notes

1. Ken Kesey, *One Flew Over the Cuckoo's Nest* (New York: Viking, 1962), p. 26. All subsequent references are to this edition and are parenthesized within the text.

2. Kurt Vonnegut, *Slaughterhouse Five* (New York: Delacorte/Seymour Lawrence, 1969), p. 33. All subsequent references are to this edition and are parenthesized within the text.

11
The Abdication
of Masculinity
in *One Flew*
Over the
Cuckoo's Nest

■■■■■■■■■■■■■■■■■■

Richard D. Maxwell

Ken Kesey, in his novel *One Flew Over the Cuckoo's Nest*, is concerned with contemporary man's loss of individuality and freedom. He seems to blame some of this on man's willingness to allow the female to take over his role, dominate him, and, as a consequence, rob him of his masculinity. The novel depicts men in a mental institution, and the ward these particular men occupy is run with an iron hand by a middle-aged, asexual woman, Big Nurse. Big Nurse's power comes, in part, from the men's refusal to stand up for their rights. She has them completely under her thumb and has stripped them of their manhood. But Big Nurse is not the only problem; she is merely taking over where others have left off. Many of the men in the asylum are there because they have permitted women to deny or cast doubts upon their masculinity. The women have done this through over-possessiveness, playing the role of mother figure, ridiculing the male's sexual prowess, becoming aggressive and sexless themselves, or denigrating sex on the grounds that it is immoral or dirty.

Originally published in *Twenty-Seven to One*, ed. Bradford C. Broughton (Ogdensburg, NY: The Ryan Press, 1970), pp. 203–11. Reprinted by permission. Copyright 1970, Clarkson University, Potsdam, NY 13676.

An example of the first type is the mother of a patient named Billy Bibbit. Billy stutters and is deathly afraid of girls, and it is easy to see why. Billy is thirty-one years old and a victim of momism. His mother works at the asylum and is a friend of Big Nurse; these two conspire to keep Billy the way he is. In fact, Billy is in the hospital for safe-keeping—he tried to desert his mother. He attempted to propose to a girl once but couldn't even do that properly because of his stutter. The stutter is, of course, simply an overt symptom of this man's total problem: the reluctance to break maternal ties for fear of offending his mother. The girl to whom he proposed couldn't suppress her laughter at his halting and ludicrous efforts to pop the question and this only served to magnify Billy's already growing fear of women. We find out why he stuttered so badly at this crucial moment. His mother thought his girlfriend was quite a bit beneath him. Billy says the fright came from being in love with the girl; however, the narrator, Chief Broom (so named because his duties consist of cleaning the ward), knows the real cause, and he tells us about an incident he witnessed. One day Billy's mother left her desk in the lobby of the hospital, took Billy by the hand and led him out to the lawn where-upon she sat down and Billy put his head in her lap. While she teased his ear with a dandelion, he talked about looking for a wife and going to college. Her reply was, "Sweetheart, you still have scads of time for things like that." To his answer that he is thirty-one years old, she laughs and says, "*Sweet*heart, do I look like the mother of a middle-aged man?"[1]

When McMurphy, the protagonist of the novel, diagnoses Billy's trouble, he tries to cure it by persuading a prostitute friend from his colorful past in the outside world to help Billy develop confidence in his manhood. After Billy finally manages to achieve satisfactory sexual relations with the girl, the couple is discovered in the act by Big Nurse. All she has to do is tell Billy how ashamed she is of his behavior and threaten to tell his mother. All the confidence he has gained in his manhood immediately drains away. She tells him how upset his mother will be. "You know how she is when she gets disturbed. Billy, you know how ill the poor woman can become. She's very sensitive. Especially concerning her son" (p. 264). After Billy, stuttering more than ever, pleads with Big Nurse not to tell, he commits suicide. This, then, is the end result of the machinations of a woman who thwarts her son's efforts to sever the umbilical cord, who tries to hold on to her youth through her son, and who denies him his normal masculine role in his relations with women.

The wife of Harding, another patient, uses different means to cause her husband concern about his masculinity. Harding not only expresses these fears openly, but indicates that all the patients are apprehensive, for one reason or another, about their abilities to function as full-fledged males. He tells McMurphy:

> . . . you are a healthy, functioning and adequate rabbit, whereas most of us in here even lack the sexual ability to make the grade as adequate rabbits. . . . We comical little creatures can't even achieve masculinity in the rabbit world, that's how weak and inadequate we are. (p. 63)

Mrs. Harding is a very amply endowed woman who continuously and in the presence of her husband flaunts her sexuality. While emphasizing her sexual assets, she denigrates Harding's potential as a man. In fact, she accuses him of having homosexual tendencies. Harding does have some feminine mannerisms of which he is aware; consequently, her accusations only serve to heighten an existing suspicion. When he is telling the story of McMurphy's battle with Big Nurse to his wife, he becomes enthusiastic and begins to use his hands to illustrate the narration. As Chief Broom tells us:

> . . . they weave the air in front of him . . . dancing the story to the tune of his voice like two beautiful ballet women in white. His hands can be anything. But as soon as the story's finished he notices McMurphy and his wife are watching the hands, and he traps them between his knees. (p. 158)

His wife plays upon his sensitive gesturing and calls attention to it, so much so that Harding can say of her, "My dear sweet but illiterate wife thinks any word or gesture that does not smack of brickyard brawn and brutality is a word or gesture of weak dandyism" (p. 44).

We only get to see this woman once, but that, combined with Harding's comments about her, is enough to let us see his problem clearly. She arrives for a visit at the asylum outside of visiting hours, but is allowed in by a ward boy who, upon leaving her with her husband, says, "Don't you forget now, you hear?" (p. 157) while she blows him a kiss, with the implication, of course, that his consideration will be rewarded at a later time. Harding introduces her to McMurphy, the epitome of her idea of masculinity, and she immediately makes a play for him, saying he shouldn't call her Mrs. Harding but Vera, again implying that she isn't a "Mrs." in the full sense of the title, that the marital tie is not a strong one, or that she is willing to ignore it. In front of McMurphy, she says to Harding, ". . . when are you going to learn to laugh instead of making that mousy little squeak?" (p. 158). Upon asking her husband for a cigarette which he cannot supply, she turns to McMurphy. "You, Mack, what about you. Can you handle a simple little thing like offering a girl a cigarette?" (p. 159). While leaning over for a light, she makes sure McMurphy can see well down into her blouse. Vera then proceeds to berate Harding because his friends are still coming around to the house. "You know the type, don't you Mack? . . . The hoity-toity boys with the nice long hair combed so perfectly and the limp little wrists that flip so nice" (p. 159). What better means to make a man who already has some doubt feel less than secure about his virility? Mrs. Harding obviously has a sexual problem as great as, if not greater than, Harding's, only she is not aware of it.

Another case in point is Chief Broom's father, to whom we are introduced through Broom's reminiscences. Although Chief Broom's real name was Bromden, this was not his father's name, and we learn how his change of names came about. The father was a big man who was reduced to a little man, partly by his wife. He was an Indian, the chief of his tribe, and he was a proud man—proud of his race, proud of his independence. He tried to stand up to the government when it wanted to destroy his village to make room for a dam. He did, too, until a combination of his own people, the whites, and his wife beat him down as a man. The Chief's Indian name was Tee Ah Millatoona, and he was proud of it. "Tee Ah Millatoona, the Pine-That-Stands-Tallest-on-the-Mountain, and I'm the biggest by God Injun in the state of Oregon and probly California and Idaho. Born right into it" (p. 239). Then he married a white woman, and she refused to take his name. "You're the biggest by God fool if you think that a good Christian woman takes on a name like Tee Ah Millatoona" (p. 239). So Chief Broom took her name instead. When they move into town, ". . . that name makes gettin' that Social Security card a lot easier" (p. 239). This was the beginning of the Chief's emasculation. Later, the government people work through Mrs. Bromden to get the

Chief to submit to their demands. A governmental representative has the idea to spread the word to the townspeople about the government's plans so they will realize there are many advantages in having a dam instead of a bunch of old shacks in their area. In addition, they type up an offer for the land and mail it to Bromden's wife instead of him, supposedly by mistake. The thinking is that it will be much easier to bring pressure on the Chief from several directions, whereas if an abrupt offer is made to Bromden they will run into "Navaho stubbornness and love of—I suppose we must call it home" (p. 182). Their scheme works and Chief Bromden ends up a broken, nameless, drunken Indian.

Big Nurse, in order to keep the men on her ward submissive to her rules and regulations, has to subdue their masculinity, which includes the urge to rebel against oppressive conditions. This is not too difficult a task with people such as Billy and Harding, who have already been partially or completely emasculated by women before they ever entered the hospital, but it is going to prove very difficult with McMurphy, who is all man. Kesey makes a point of McMurphy's masculinity. He is a redheaded Irishman, broad across the jaw, shoulders and chest, with a scar received in a fight slanting across his nose and cheekbone. He has been a logging bum, a wanderer, and a gambler. A doctor at a jail work farm told him that he was a psychopath, which means, says McMurphy, attempting to put it delicately in mixed company, that he is over*zealous* in his sexual relations (p. 46). What is more, in addition to these masculine attributes, he says he has never seen a woman he thought was more man than he. Thus we have the challenge and the challenger. As Harding says:

> . . . *man has but* one *truly effective weapon against the*
> *juggernaut of modern matriarchy.* . . . *One weapon, and*
> *with every passing year in this hip, motivationally*
> *researched society, more and more people are discovering*
> *how to render that weapon useless and conquer those who*
> *have hitherto been the conquerors. (p. 66)*

This weapon is male virility. McMurphy has it and will use it to try to rectify a situation in which this weapon has become useless, because the other men are unsure they possess it.

Against McMurphy and what he stands for, Big Nurse will use every weapon in the female arsenal. Like Harding's wife, she will use ridicule. Like Billy's mother, she will use momism, treating grown men like children. To these tactics she will add a few of her own.

One of her favorite devices is the group therapy sessions in which she encourages the men to outdo each other in revealing their own and each other's faults. When they do this, she is in her element because she can later use this information to strengthen her advantage over the men.

> *It was better than she'd dreamed. They were all shouting to outdo one another, going further and further, no way of stopping, telling things that wouldn't ever let them look one another in the eye again. The Nurse nodding at each confession and saying, Yes, yes, yes. (p. 49)*

McMurphy calls these sessions "peckin' parties," comparing them to that chicken yard phenomenon wherein the chickens see a spot of blood on one chicken and all start pecking at it until they rip the chicken to shreds. He says it is Big Nurse, in this case, who pecks that first peck, and she is not pecking at a spot of blood.

> *That's not what she's peckin' at. . . . [She pecks] right at your balls. No, that nurse ain't some kinda monster chicken, buddy, what she is is a ball cutter. I've seen thousands of 'em, old and young, men and women. Seen 'em all over the country and in the homes—people who try to make you weak so they can get you to toe the line, to follow their rules, to live like they want you to. And the best way to do this, to get you to knuckle under, is to weaken you by gettin' you where it hurts the worst. . . . And that's what that old buzzard is doing, going for your vitals. (p. 57)*

That is exactly what Big Nurse is doing. If she can make a man less than a man she can control him, and any method she can use to do this will be employed.

She uses this tactic not only inside the ward, but on all men. I think we can, perhaps, see what motivates this hostility toward men. A special point is made of her lack of sexuality, especially in reference to her breasts, which she tries to conceal. They detract from the authoritarian image she wishes to convey most of the time. "A mistake was made somehow in manufacturing, putting those big womanly breasts on what would of otherwise been a perfect work, and you can see how bitter she is about it" (p. 11). She only adopts the female role when she knows it to be her most effective method of dealing with a particular patient. At all other times she is sexless, even rather masculine in her stern efficiency. No trace of femininity is displayed. Apparently she feels this would make her vulnerable. Indeed, McMurphy's last act, before a lobotomy is performed upon him, is to expose her as a female. This revelation serves to lessen her ability to enforce her regime with an iron hand, as she formerly did.

> *Only at the last—after he'd smashed through that glass*
> *door, her face swinging around, with terror forever*
> *ruining any other look she might ever try to use again,*
> *screaming when he grabbed for her and ripped her*
> *uniform all the way down the front, screaming again*
> *when the two nippled circles started from her chest and*
> *swelled out and out. . . . (p. 267)*

When she returns from the hospital after McMurphy's manhandling, the patients grin at the front of her new uniform. It is smaller and tighter, even more starched than her old one, but ". . . it could no longer conceal the fact that she was a woman" (p. 268). What has caused her to become what she is? It seems that she is sexually frustrated. Since she has not been allowed to function as a woman sexually, she has obliterated all her female characteristics and has directed this frustration toward all males. Another nurse, after a particular bit of cruelty aimed at the men by Big Nurse, hints at her perversity. "Army nurses, trying to run an Army hospital. They are a little sick themselves. I sometimes think all single nurses should be fired after they reach thirty-five" (p. 234). This hostility is in evidence at all times, not only during working hours. She visits a newlywed couple in town with a basket of groceries because they are in difficult financial straits. Upon leaving, she takes the bride aside and gives her twenty dollars, saying, "Go, you poor unfortunate underfed child, go, and buy yourself a *decent* dress. I *realize* your husband can't afford it, but here, take this, and *go*" (p. 58). This belittling of the husband's ability as provider is emasculation in one of its more viciously subtle, or perhaps not-so-subtle, forms.

A common practice of people not capable of sexual enjoyment or finding sexual partners themselves is to assert that sexual activity is immoral or dirty in some way. Big Nurse assumes this stance. When McMurphy succeeds in replacing the *McCall's* magazines, which always adorned the reading room, with men's magazines, Big Nurse refers to the pictures of girls clipped from them and hung on the walls as pornography from smut books. She also plans to see that an investigation is made concerning the "dirt" brought into the hospital. When Billy and the prostitute are discovered, she says she is ashamed of him for associating with this "cheap! low! painted" woman. Kesey, however, indicates why Big Nurse has this attitude. The prostitute is meant to be a foil for Big Nurse. Just as he emphasizes McMurphy's masculinity, he stresses this girl's feminity. She is like a breath of fresh air when she enters the ward. She is all woman, knows it and enjoys it. She is proud of her womanhood and likes nothing better than to feel men's eyes upon her. She is a perfect contrast to Big Nurse. Chief Broom expresses all the men's impressions of her on her first appearance.

> *She was younger and prettier than any of us'd figured on*
> *. . . seeing her coming lightfooted across the grass with*
> *her eyes green all the way up to the ward, and her hair,*
> *roped in a long twist at the back of her head, jouncing up*
> *and down with every step like copper springs in the sun,*
> *all any of us could think of was that she was a girl, a*
> *female who wasn't dressed white from head to foot like*
> *she's been dipped in frost, and how she made her money*
> *didn't make any difference. (p. 195)*

For females who want to make sex dirty or who are sexless or sexually frustrated, a woman who exudes sex in this manner is anathema.

Big Nurse also likes to make men feel incapable. She can always manage to find fault with something. Even the doctor on the ward, hand-picked by Big Nurse, is ". . . completely conscious of his inadequacy. He's a frightened, desperate, ineffectual little rabbit, totally incapable of running this ward without our Miss Ratched's [Big Nurse's] help, and he knows it" (p. 59). Harding says she has a genius for insinuation. She never has accused him directly of anything, but he *feels* she has accused him of jealousy, paranoia, not being man enough to satisfy his wife, and having relations with males (p. 60). Chief Broom notices what she does to Billy and feels helpless under the circumstances: she taunts Billy for his being frightened of the girl to whom he tried to propose. Under the guise of trying to help, but actually adding to his feelings of inadequacy, she asks him what it was about this girl that frightened him so. Chief Broom can only observe and comment: "And as far as the nurse riding you like this, rubbing your nose in your weakness till what little dignity you got left is gone and you shrink up to nothing from humiliation, I can't do anything about that either" (p. 121).

Finally, Big Nurse and Billy's mother are two of a kind. Both women treat Billy like a child, thus causing him to feel like a child, incapable of making his own decisions and forced to remain dependent on the mother figure. Big Nurse only uses her sex when she wants to appear maternal. A few examples will suffice. One of her favorite lectures to the inmates concerns their not being able to adjust to the rules of society. She tells them that although they were able to get away with this as children, they knew when they had broken a rule and wanted to be punished. Big Nurse concludes that this need for discipline they didn't receive was the germ of their present illness. Using the same words that all mothers have always used, she says, "I tell you this hoping you will understand that it is *entirely for your own good* that we enforce discipline and order" (p. 171). In other words, Big Nurse, as the mother to these grown men, will chastise them when she feels they need it. This is evident in her reaction upon discovering Billy and the prostitute. "'William Bibbit!' She tried so hard to sound cold and stern. 'William . . . Bibbit'" (p. 263). Billy breaks down. "She . . . drew his cheek to her starched breast, stroking his shoulder while she turned a slow, contemptuous look across the bunch of us" (p. 265). She then led him toward her office saying "Poor boy, poor little boy" (p. 265).

Using the hospital ward, the patients, and Big Nurse as his microcosm, Kesey seems to attribute at least part of modern man's dilemma to his relinquishment of the traditional role of the dominant male. We have always had dominant females among us, just as we have always had some men willing to play a subservient role. We have also always had the types of women Kesey portrays—the over-possessive mother, the predatory or aggressive female. However, I think Kesey is warning us that some recent developments in American society may serve to weaken masculine individuality, assertiveness, and spirit. It is only in the twentieth century that women in large numbers have become financially independent. Competing with men in the world of commerce has made them necessarily more aggressive and competitive. In addition, when the male has lost the role of sole provider, he has lost a large part of his traditional image. Other factors also compromise traditional masculine roles and values. The struggle to get ahead in our highly materialistic society has forced men to spend more time away from their families, and as a result they have turned over to their wives many of their former duties, such as those of chief disciplinarian, keeper of the budget, and general master of the house. Corporations are demanding more than loyalty from employees who must maintain the proper image. How masculine is the man who lets his company deny him a beard if he wishes one? How can a man assert his individuality and maintain his integrity if he has to give in to his employer's wishes in order to maintain a home, two cars, a boat, and a snowmobile?

It is apparent that Kesey is not putting the entire blame on women. In many cases the woman dominates the man because he lets her. It is the male who is allowing the female and the corporation to chip away at his masculinity. The man who gives away his responsibilities or his individuality in exchange for material comforts has also given away some of his masculinity. The woman who competes with a man in what previously was his private arena loses some of her femininity and is bound to become more aggressive. Kesey is telling us that once a certain amount of masculinity in the form of authority and individuality is yielded, it is difficult to regain. Perhaps men have given away too much.

Notes

1. Ken Kesey, *One Flew Over the Cuckoo's Nest* (New York: Signet, 1962), p. 247. All quotations and references will be from this edition.

12
The Big Nurse
as Ratchet:
Sexism in
Kesey's
Cuckoo's Nest

◆◆◆◆◆◆◆◆◆◆◆◆◆◆

Elizabeth McMahan

Ken Kesey's *One Flew Over the Cuckoo's Nest* is a good novel—a really teachable novel. Students get caught up in it and are eager to talk about the characters and to explore the ramifications of the partial allegory. But despite these positive qualities, *Cuckoo's Nest* is a sexist novel. Certainly I don't want to discourage anyone from teaching it, but I do urge that colleagues should present the novel in a way that will disclose its concealed sexist bias. In order to get at the invidious aspect of *Cuckoo's Nest*, let me review the way Kesey structures his microcosm.

The novel offers a compelling presentation of the way society manipulates individuals in order to keep the bureaucracy running smoothly. The mental hospital is "a little world Inside that is a made to scale prototype of the big world Outside,"[1] with both worlds being operated by the Combine, Chief Broom's appropriate name for the Establishment. A combine is a group united to pursue commercial or political interests and is also a machine that cuts off and chews up

Originally published in the *College English Association Critic* 37: 4 (1975), pp. 25–27. Reprinted by permission of College English Association Publications.

and spits out a product. Kesey has fused both meanings in his image, with the by-product being *us*—the members of society.

Boss of that "factor for the Combine" is the Big Nurse, the embodiment of the castrating female. If you're old enough to remember Philip Wylie's *Generation of Vipers*, you have met the Big Nurse before: she is Mom. Wylie described her this way:

> *She is a middle-aged puffin with an eye like a hawk that has just seen a rabbit twitch far below. She is about twenty-five pounds overweight . . . with sharp heels and a hard backhand which she does not regard as a foul but a womanly defense. In a thousand of her there is not sex appeal enough to budge a hermit ten paces off a rock ledge.*[2]

You remember good old Mom. Kesey calls her Miss Ratched and thus acknowledges her role as a tool of the Combine. A ratchet is a mechanism that engages the teeth of a wheel permitting motion in one direction only. Kesey's metaphor is perfect. The ward is littered with casualties of "momism": Billy Bibbit's stuttering began with his first word, M-m-m-m-mama; Ruckley's only utterance throughout the novel is "Ffffuck da wife"; Harding's neurosis stems from inferiority feelings agitated by his wife's "ample bosom"; Chief Broom's self-concept shrank in sympathy with his once-powerful father after, he says, "my mother made him too little to fight any more and he gave up" (p. 187). McMurphy, on the other hand, has escaped the controls of the Combine because he has "no wife wanting new linoleum" (p. 84).

Kesey's eye is accurate in his depiction of this microcosm. The ward hums along on beams of fear and hate. The black boys are clearly serving the Combine in order to wreak vengeance on their white oppressors. The best hater of the bunch, "a dwarf the color of cold asphalt," peered from a closet at age five to watch his mother's rape, "while his papa stood by tied to the hot iron stove with plow traces, blood streaming into his shoes" (p. 31). Kesey makes his point melodramatically clear: the blacks are portrayed as villains because society has victimized them. They are merely retaliating.

But why is the Big Nurse so eager to emasculate the men in her charge? Why does *she* serve as a dedicated tool of the Combine? This is a question Kesey never answers; he apparently never thinks to ask it. He understands and castigates the injustice of prejudice against Indians. Remember how Chief Broom developed his habit of feigning deaf and dumbness: it was his response to people, he says, "that first started acting like I was too dumb to hear or see or say anything at all" (p. 178). You recall how the Indians are conned out of their homes and their way of life by the sneering, deprecating white people from town. Kesey shows himself sympathetic to oppressed minorities in our society. But what about our oppressed majority?

It never seems to occur to Kesey that possibly the Big Nurse relishes her job as "ball cutter" for precisely the same reason that the black boys take pleasure in their work. But anyone who has read Germain Greer's *The Female Eunuch* can see in the novel the fulfillment of the biblical injunction: an eye for an eye, a tooth for a tooth, a castration for a castration. Philip Wylie thirty years ago observed that "the mealy look of men today is the result of momism and so is the pinched and baffled fury in the eyes of womankind" (p. 199). True, perhaps. But Wylie thought the solution to the problem was to force woman back into her proper subservient place where she wold become content again—like those happy slaves on the plantation, I suppose. And you remember Kesey's solution: Harding suggests that "man has only *one* truly effective weapon against the juggernaut of modern matriarchy." But even our virile hero McMurphy confesses that there's no way he could "get a bone up over that old buzzard." "There you are," says Harding. "She's won" (p. 66).

Women, you notice, keep winning these sexual battles—according to the men who manufacture them. Truth is, *nobody* wins—certainly not women. Consider how women are portrayed in Kesey's novel. We've already noted examples of the castrating bitch—Nurse Ratched, Mrs. Bibbit, Mrs. Harding, and Mrs. Bromden. Then we have the little nurse who hates the patients because her weak mind has been so warped by the Church that she thinks her birthmark a stain visited upon her because of her association with the depraved inmates. And there is the townswoman with the eyes that "spring up like the numbers in a cash register" (p. 182), who dupes the Indians by negotiating with *Mrs.* Bromden, rather than dealing with the Chief.

You may ask, are there no *good* women in Kesey's estimation? Well, yes. There is the nurse on the Disturbed Ward, an angel of mercy by virtue of ethnic origin—the little Japanese nurse. She accepts woman's time-honored role as nurturer of men and agrees with

McMurphy that sexual starvation prompts Miss Ratched's perversity. "I sometimes think," she says, "all single nurses should be fired after they reach thirty-five" (p. 234). A sympathetic woman—to men, at least.

And there is also Candy, the whore with a heart of gold, and her friend, Sandy, who is equally charitable with her body. These women ask nothing of the men—not even money for their sexual performances. Kesey fantasizes that they come willingly to this insane asylum to service the inmates for the sheer joy of it. In his euphoric state, Chief Broom marvels:

> Drunk and running and laughing and carrying on with
> women square in the center of the Combine's most
> powerful stronghold! . . . I had to remind myself that it
> had truly happened, that we had made it happen. We had
> just unlocked a window and let it in like you let in the
> fresh air. Maybe the Combine wasn't so all-powerful.
> (p. 255)

What came in through the window "like fresh air"? The two prostitutes. Kesey implies that if all women would just behave generously like Candy and Sandy, the Combine might then become vulnerable.

Kesey, I think, is wrong about the way to loosen the stranglehold of the emasculating female and break up the Combine. He is simply visionary to suggest that women should emulate the attitude of the happy hookers. The truth is that women are not likely at this point to give up bossing their men around when this remains their only means of achieving a semblance of importance in society. Yet I agree with Ann Nietzke that

> contrary to popular belief, women do not want to castrate
> men; it's just that we are tired of being eunuchs
> ourselves. This does not mean that women want penises
> but that we want the powers, freedoms, and dignities that
> are automatically granted to the people who happen to
> have them.[3]

If the Combine could be subverted to the extent of giving up its ratchet—of allowing women genuine equality—then women could stop emasculating men and turn their energies to more self-fulfilling pursuits. Given the opportunity to run that ward in her own right, instead of having to manipulate the rabbity doctor, perhaps Miss Ratched might have run it more humanely. Forcing people into deviousness can hardly be expected to improve their character. And inequality is almost guaranteed to generate malice.

Thus we need to help students see that Nurse Ratched is no more to blame for her malice than the black boys are for theirs. The Big Nurse happens also to be the Big Victim when viewed with an awareness of the social and economic exploitation of women. Kesey didn't have exactly this in mind, I grant, but we can still derive this insight from his novel and correct the damaging impression that the book leaves—that women, through some innate perversity, are the cause of all of society's failings.

Notes

1. Ken Kesey, *One Flew Over the Cuckoo's Nest* (New York: Signet, 1962), pp. 48–49. All references are to this edition.

2. Philip Wylie, *Generation of Vipers* (New York: Pocket Books, 1942, 1955), p. 191. All references are to this edition.

3. Ann Nietzke, "Hostility on the Laugh Track," *Human Behavior* 3 (May 1974), p. 66.

13

"It's the Truth Even If It Didn't Happen": Ken Kesey's *One Flew Over the Cuckoo's Nest*

•••••••••••••••

Elaine B. Safer

Ken Kesey's *One Flew over the Cuckoo's Nest* (first published in 1962) has sold millions of paperback copies and been particularly popular with college students. The hero, Randle Patrick McMurphy, epitomizes, especially for the young, a nonconformist's struggle against the oppressive social system. The mental ward's patients—the Acutes, the Chronics, the Vegetables—have counterparts outside the hospital. The hospital's hierarchical power structure—with the Big Nurse as castrator at its top—reflects the cold, calculating machinations of a repressive society that disregards civil rights and destroys individuality.

In 1963, David Merrick and Edward Lewis produced Dale Wasserman's dramatized version of *Cuckoo's Nest* at the Cort Theatre, and Kirk Douglas starred as Randle P. McMurphy. I did not see this early dramatization, but I did see the later production of Wasserman's play when it opened off-Broadway in 1971 at the Mercer-Hansberry The-

Originally published in *Literature/Film Quarterly* 5: 2 (1977), pp. 132–41. Reprinted by permission. Copyright 1977, Salisbury State University, Salisbury, MD 21801.

atre, where applauding young audiences rooted for McMurphy as he struggled against Nurse Ratched, agent of the Combine.[1] More recently, a film version of *Cuckoo's Nest* was adapted by screen writers Lawrence Hauben and Bo Goldman and directed by Milos Forman, starring Jack Nicholson as McMurphy and Louise Fletcher as the Big Nurse. The film won five Oscars at the Academy Awards, including best screenplay adapted from another medium. This was the first time since 1934 that one film got all the major awards: best picture, best actor, best actress, and best director.

Most critics have praised the movie for its realism and comic sensibility, but also have criticized its absence of "the nightmare quality that made the book a capsulized allegory of an increasingly mad reality."[2] The film audience stamped and cheered McMurphy as he battled the terrors of the mental hospital. But only the novel transforms the horrors of the mental ward into a microcosm of the complex suppression exercised by society upon its dissident members.

Ken Kesey—in a 1970 interview in *Rolling Stone*—expressed his wish to make a film of *Cuckoo's Nest*: "I could do it weird. I could do it so that people, when they left there, they couldn't find the exit. Direct it. Direct it and write it."[3] Kesey's inclination to "do it weird" is at the opposite pole from the Milos Forman movie, which accentuates realism. The film is set in Oregon State Hospital at Salem, a large, impersonal-looking group of buildings, with high fences, window-locked screens outside every room, stark locked wards, large sleeping rooms devoid of privacy, and limited activity areas. The camera's eye focuses on repeated lineups of patients for medication, therapeutic community sessions, strong aides restraining patients, and electric shock treatment. Especially realistic is the administration of shock treatment with such particulars as the mouth gag, electrodes placed on each side of the head, the convulsions, and the facial discoloration of the patient. Forman details the sordid and also the comic aspects of a "cuckoo's nest," where physical aberrations reflect psychological ones. The stuttering Billy Bibbit becomes painful to watch. Other patients are comic representatives of a "loony bin": the huge zombie, Taber; the short, fat Martini; the paraplegic colonel in the wheelchair hitting a punching bag with his cane; the catatonic who, during McMurphy's wild party, has liquor squirted into his mouth from an enema tube; and the patient who dances about endlessly. Casting was crucial for Milos Forman. "Since the patients in the mental ward have few lines to say, [the] audience must remember each simply by their look."[4]

Comic realism is the forte of Milos Forman. It was evident in his earlier films, *Loves of a Blonde, The Fireman's Ball,* and *Taking Off.*[5] *Cuckoo's Nest,* under Forman's direction, focuses on the conflict between the Big Nurse and McMurphy—the agent of society as opposed to its dissident member. Kesey's surreal prose is converted into concrete detailed scenes. Particularly detailed are the facial expressions of Nurse Ratched (Louise Fletcher) and Randle P. McMurphy (Jack Nicholson).[6] The camera's eye focuses on Louise Fletcher's controlled gradation of facial expressions: the closed-lipped smile of satisfaction, the firmer set line of righteous concern, the slight shade of impatience or anger or hatred, and the cold eyes. The camera also follows Jack Nicholson, the rebel who exchanges a prison work farm for a mental institution. The camera's eye catches his zany antics as he walks into the mental hospital and makes faces at the patients peering down at him. McMurphy is as uncontrolled as the Big Nurse is controlled. He Indian-whoops upon meeting Chief Bromden; has a sparkle in his eye; an open smile for all; and an energetic, eager expression when possibilities for pranks arise. As the movie progresses, the smile often turns to surprise and outrage and strain, and also to the tight-lipped expression of calm acceptance, as McMurphy matches wits with Nurse Ratched in therapeutic community sessions. At the close, McMurphy's face is denuded of all expression, a graphic representation of the "open and undreaming [eyes] . . . like smudged fuses in a fuse box."[7]

Kesey, in writing the novel, exulted in the use of images that are conveyed by the narrator, a schizophrenic inpatient. Kesey saw Bromden's perspective as "extremely difficult to pull off," a perspective that "fair makes the mind real [sic]."[8] The nightmare quality of the novel grows out of Bromden's consciousness, where abstract concepts take on concrete manifestations,[9] where the machinelike Big Nurse "blows up bigger and bigger, big as a tractor" (p. 11). Bromden's story, we feel is "the truth even if it didn't happen" (p. 13).

Playwright Dale Wasserman preserved much of the narration of Bromden, the schizophrenic through whose eyes all details are filtered. The soundtrack was played at intervals throughout the drama, revealing Bromden's perspective. Bromden appeared on a darkened stage with a shaft of light on him:

> *Papa? They're foggin' it in again. Somethin' bad is gonna*
> *happen, so they're foggin' it in. . . . You hear it, Papa?*
> *The Black Machine. . . . They're puttin' people in one*
> *end and out comes what they want. . . . You think I'm*
> *ravin' 'cause it sounds too awful to be true, but, my God,*
> *there's such a lot of things that's true even if they never*
> *really happen!*[10]

Forman, in the movie, has supplanted Bromden's interior mon-
ologue with concrete detailed scenes. He has exchanged surreal description for realistic presentation of patients in an institutional setting.
In this setting, Forman develops scenes which stress comic realism.
It is for laughs that Forman expands and changes scenes in which
the *machismo* hero, McMurphy, excels: the Monopoly game in which
McMurphy squirts the men with water; the wild party with hard
liquor and women; the basketball game in which McMurphy gets the
slow six-foot-eight-inch Bromden to drop the team's ball into a basket
and pop out the opponents' ball; McMurphy's escape over the hospital
yard's wire fence; his run into a Big Yellow Bus, which he drives
away; and the patients' commandeering of a boat for a rollicking good
time at sea. McMurphy, the rebellious savior of Kesey's novel, becomes McMurphy, the rable rouser and prankster. Jack Nicholson
plays McMurphy as an imaginative, attractive, sympathetic hustler,
a clever guy who chooses the mental institution as a means to evade
the work farm to which he had been sentenced, a man who easily
gains control of incapacitated men in a cuckoo's nest; he is a *machismo*
hero, but not a mythic one.

It is from Bromden's perspective (in the novel) that McMurphy
gains mythic proportions as he heroically defies the dark terrors inherent in the institutional setting. For Bromden, the hospital system
controls all behavior by means of hidden machinery, which accelerates
or slows down time, fills the air with fog, and turns men into machines. The patients, from Bromden's perspective, are fearful rabbits
("Billy Bibbit and Cheswick change into hunched-over white rabbits,
right before my eyes" [p. 61]) as well as lifeless machines, "machines
with flaws inside that can't be repaired, flaws born in, or flaws beat
in over so many years . . . bleeding rust" (p. 19). For Bromden, the
domineering Miss Ratched is a creature sitting in the center of wires,
controlling everything "with mechanical insect skill" (p. 30). In turn,

she is a Circean creature, carrying a bag filled with magical devices to transform patients as she pleases, such as "tiny pills that gleam like porcelain, needles, forceps" (p. 10), and a Medusan figure with petrifying power to freeze all who disobey her, like Billy Bibbit, who looks "only straight ahead at her face, like there was a spiraling light there . . . a hypnotizing swirl" (pp. 264–65)—a powerful beam, as well as a huge machine, "crooking . . . sectioned arms" (p. 11) around patients.

From Bromden's perspective, the action revolves around the struggle between the phantasmagorical destroyer, Nurse Ratched, and the redeemer, Randle P. McMurphy. McMurphy offers the oppressed the possibility of a rebirth. In Bromden's eyes, he is a mythical hero: a boisterous gambler, fighter, lover of wine and women, a robust cowboy of the American West whose iron "boot heels cracked lightning out of the tile" (p. 172), as well as a Christ figure whose strength raises the men from their fear and inertia. Shock treatment is given to McMurphy on a table shaped like a cross, emitting a "crown of electric sparks in place of thorns" (p. 65). Bromden hopes McMurphy will diminish the power of evil: the malevolent Big Nurse, her three black aides who appear like apparitions in their white suits, and the callous hospital personnel who commit atrocities that even cause inanimate objects to weep—"table legs strained and contorted and the chairs knotted and the walls gritted against one another till you could of wrung sweat out of the room" (p. 131). Bromden's weird vision accumulates details that spiral upward to mythic proportions of good and evil, Christ and the Devil. Notice, for example, the significance Bromden attributes to the day's outing arranged by McMurphy. From Bromden's perspective, the outing provides psychological growth for the men. At sea, away from the restraints of the Big Nurse and the Combine, they follow the lead of McMurphy. They are gradually enabled to laugh at their predicament, at the whole human predicament. Bromden notes mishaps in steering the boat, cranking in the fish, and adjusting to the presence of McMurphy's girlfriend. He observes the mishaps and finds himself laughing: "laughing at the girl, at the guys, at George, at me sucking my bleeding thumb" (pp. 211–12). Bromden finally appreciates the complex nature of the humor encouraged by McMurphy: McMurphy "won't let the pain blot out the humor no more'n he'll let the humor blot out the pain" (p. 212). From Bromden's perspective, McMurphy's twelve followers grow physically and spiritually as they appreciate the humor and pain of the human predicament:

> *It started slow and pumped itself full, swelling the men bigger and bigger. I watched, part of them, laughing with them—and somehow not with them. I was off the boat, blown up off the water and skating the wind with those black birds, high above myself, and I could look down and see myself and the rest of the guys, see the boat rocking there in the middle of those diving birds, see McMurphy surrounded by his dozen people, and watch them, us, swinging a laughter that rang out on the water in ever-widening circles, farther and farther, until it crashed up on beaches all over the coast, on beaches all over all coasts, in wave after wave after wave. (p. 212)*

In the movie, this psychological growth—the ability to perceive the dimensions of humor in pain and pain in humor—is forfeited for the one-dimensional level of slapstick humor, befitting a scene in which men from a "nut house" take over a stolen boat. Milos Forman emphasizes a fast moving pace, the tension involved in violating the law, the blundering on the boat, and the humorous pranks of the men. The camera's eye moves quickly from the commandeered boat recklessly circling about without anyone at the helm, narrowly avoiding one mishap after another, to police helicopters above, and finally to the arrival at shore where police are waiting to receive the men.

The same technique of thinning down the pain and humor of a situation to the level of slapstick is evident in the scene in which Bromden finally breaks his twenty years of silence in order to communicate with McMurphy. In the novel, the hospital aide shows McMurphy Bromden's hiding place for gum—the underside of his mattress: "You see, for years I been wondering where Chief Bromden got his chewin' gum—never havin' any money for the canteen, never havin' anybody give him a stick that I saw . . . so I *watched*, and I *waited*" (p. 184). When the aide leaves, McMurphy sings a hillbilly song: "Oh, does the Spearmint lose its flavor on the bedpost overnight?" And Bromden, gradually seeing the humor in the situation, laughs at his own predicament. Encouraged by McMurphy's concern and kindness, Bromden breaks his twenty years of silence and thanks his hero:

It didn't sound like much because my throat was rusty
and my tongue creaked. He told me I sounded a little out
of practice and laughed at that. I tried to laugh with him,
but it was a squawking sound, like a pullet trying to
crow. It sounded more like crying than laughing. (p. 185)

Filtered through Bromden's consciousness at this point are the painful reasons behind his twenty years of silence: his sense of inadequacy starting when his father, an Indian Chief, is reduced in stature by his white wife; the fact that the Combine made the Chief sign away the tribe, the village, and the land, and gave him money for cars that he could not drive and alcohol which destroyed his moral fiber: "It sucks out of him until he's shrunk so wrinkled and yellow even the dogs don't know him" (p. 188). Such negative experiences have caused Bromden to withdraw from people for twenty years. McMurphy's sensitivity to Bromden's need and also his appreciation of the comic elements in the Chief's condition—and the human condition—encourage Bromden to rise out of his deaf-and-dumb silence.

In the movie, Milos Forman collapses the above scene to a swift interchange between McMurphy and Bromden as they await their turn to have electric shock treatment. McMurphy offers Bromden a stick of gum, is taken aback by Bromden's "Thank you," and the audience, in turn, delights in the Chief's next words after twenty years of silence: "Juicy Fruit."

An essential part of the novel is the focus on McMurphy as role model for Bromden and the other patients. It is through his faith in McMurphy—Bromden's desire "to touch him because he's who he is" (pp. 188)—that Bromden experiences a rebirth. As McMurphy's effectiveness increases, Chief Bromden rises to fuller stature; the fog circulating around people and surroundings begins to recede, allowing him to look outside the hospital window at nature (p. 142) instead of withdrawing into himself. He no longer views his fellow patients as machines without blood or innards, "just a shower of rust and ashes" (p. 81), and he gains inner strength so that he eventually lifts the unliftable control panel and smashes it through the mesh wire outside the window, "baptizing the sleeping earth" (pp. 271–72). The relationship between Bromden and McMurphy is thus central to the novel, which is as much about Bromden's gradual affirmation of life as it is about McMurphy's conflict with the Big Nurse.

By transferring the point of view from Bromden's imagistic rum-
inations to objective presentation, Milos Forman causes the audience
to observe all action from the outside rather than from within. Bromden's growing respect for McMurphy and his gradual loss of fear and
new desire for life are only portrayed pictorially. In effect, the movie
emphasizes only one major part of the book: McMurphy's challenge
of the establishment, represented by Nurse Ratched. We are appalled
by the gruesome details of lobotomy and electric shock treatment—
weapons of the Big Nurse; we cheer the hero on in his fight, laugh
at his antics as he razzes the Big Nurse, parades through the mess
hall in unusual dress, or squirts water at patients playing Monopoly;
but without Bromden's sensitive perspective, we also laugh at the
weird patients. McMurphy represents "a man from the real world
entering the looney bin."[11] We are the *sane* observers of a "cuckoo's
nest"; we are outside, not inside, Bromden's perspective.

In the novel, hyperbole is used to show how Bromden, the other
patients, and the hospital staff fear the Big Nurse, agent of the Combine: "She's swelling up, swells till her back's splitting out the white
uniform and she's let her arms section out long enough to wrap
around the three of them" (p. 11). In the film, Nurse Ratched seems
shorn of mythic associations. She is no longer a huge machine or a
witch or a Circean figure but an authoritative nurse called Mildred,
a woman who gives a strong professional appearance in her handling
of the ward. In the film, Mildred exhibits controlled tone and gestures,
tight-lipped smile, excellent diction and clear sentences, and—above
all—concern that the ward be run by her supreme guidance. Milos
Forman perceives her as "not sadistical, only fanatical."[12] Louise Fletcher
has managed, as Charles Champlin recently observed, "to be monstrous but not a monster, hateful but not grotesque, the very model
of the good citizen doing the job, disastrously."[13] Her coolness, deliberateness, and inflexible stance of professionalism are destructive,
but she is not a mythic creation. Nurse Ratched, as played by Louise
Fletcher, lacks mercy and compassion. Because of her fanaticism, she
is "blind to her own anger and love of power, squelching her patients'
manhood with the blandest of smiles."[14] But Nurse Ratched lacks the
complexities of Kesey's fantasy: she is no metaphoric demon come
to life, and she does not represent the castrating female of archetypal
proportions.[15] Forman's realism has reduced her to "a handsome,

hard-faced, flat-voiced, infinitely patient"[16] nurse, whose controlling behavior has disastrous consequences.

This thinning of character is part of an overall simplification of dimension in Forman's film script. At the conclusion of the film, Bromden crashes the control panel through the hospital's mesh wire screen and window. The act graphically shows that he has succeeded in overcoming the destructive power of the institution. He has broken away from the confines of the hospital. He is free. Through McMurphy's efforts, Bromden has attained a new life.

In the book, however, such exhilaration is more complex:

> *I ran across the grounds in the direction I remembered*
> *seeing the dog go, toward the highway. I remember I was*
> *taking huge strides as I ran, seeming to step and float a*
> *long ways before my next foot struck the earth. I felt like*
> *I was flying. Free. (p. 272)*

Bromden feels rejuvenated: "The glass splashed . . . like a bright cold water baptizing the sleeping earth" (pp. 271–72). McMurphy, we believe, has died as savior for Bromden and the men.[17] Bromden seems to float through the window. He wishes to return to the pure land of his childhood before it was corrupted by the white man. He wants the excitement of living close to nature—spearing salmon as they go over the falls. Bromden's joy at the conclusion of the novel is similar to his sense of rejuvenation on the sea voyage with McMurphy, away from the restraints of the hospital and the Combine. It is similar to the joy he experienced in childhood.

This passage is most interesting for the reader of *Cuckoo's Nest* because it is the only time in the novel that we can see beyond Bromden's perspective. Bromden, in his exhilaration, recalls the dog he had seen loping in the breeze under a moonlit sky. The dog had been intoxicated with his freedom: "The night, the breeze full of smells so wild makes a young dog drunk" (p. 142). Above the loping dog Canada honkers are flying. The dog runs in the direction of the Canada honkers, toward the highway. Bromden observes, "I watched the dog and the car making for the same spot of pavement" (p. 143).

Bromden, at the close of the novel, recalls the loping dog but represses the fact that the dog was headed for destruction. In his optimism, he only remembers the movement toward freedom. Placement of the suggestive imagery of the dog gives the reader the advantage of recalling the information Bromden has repressed:

> *The dog could still hear them a long time after me. He*
> *was still standing with his paw up; he hadn't moved or*
> *barked when they flew over. When he couldn't hear them*
> *any more either, he commenced to lope off in the direction*
> *they had gone, toward the highway, loping steady and*
> *solemn like he had an appointment. I held my breath and*
> *I could hear the flap of his big paws on the grass as he*
> *loped: then I could hear a car speed up out of a turn. The*
> *headlights loomed over the rise and peered ahead down*
> *the highway. I watched the dog and the car making for*
> *the same spot of pavement. (p. 143)*

The suggestive imagery of the dog presents the complexity of Kesey's thrust, the underlying pessimism, which Bromden had once appreciated as he watched McMurphy—under strain—play out his role as hero for the men: "The thing he [McMurphy] was fighting, you couldn't whip it for good. All you could do was keep on whipping it, till you couldn't come out any more and somebody else had to take your place" (p. 265). The underlying pessimism stresses the connection between the oppressiveness of the mental hospital and that of society as a whole—the fact that "the ward is a factory for the Combine, . . . for fixing up mistakes made in the neighborhoods and in the schools and in the churches" (p. 40) and that the regimentation of the hospital is reflected in society, where people live in "five thousand houses punched out identical by a machine" (p. 203).

Bromden leaps toward freedom, exulting in a joyous reassertion of his Indian past. The novel juxtaposes Bromden's ecstatic movement toward freedom (following in the footsteps of McMurphy) with our foreboding (caused by the suggestive cross reference) that he, like the dog loping in the breeze, will be destroyed. The ending leaves the reader frustrated, entangled in the polarities of rebirth and destruction, freedom and oppression, hope and despair. Had Milos Forman used Bromden as narrator instead of employing objective narration, and had he used surreal details instead of realistic ones—i.e., had he done it "weird," following Ken Kesey's lead—he might have caused the cinema audience to be so shocked and distraught "when they left there, they couldn't find the exit."[18]

Notes

1. Walter Kerr observes: "These young men and women . . . have come to attend to an image of what they most fear in their lives . . . that 'conditioning' which is the central action of the play," in "And the Young Flew over the Cuckoo's Nest," Ken Kesey, *One Flew Over the Cuckoo's Nest*, ed. John Clark Pratt (New York: Viking Press, 1973), p. 447; orig. pub., *The New York Times*, 1971.

2. Jack Kroll, "You're All Right, Jack," *Newsweek*, 24 November 1975, p. 113.

3. Kesey is interviewed by Michael Goodwin, "The Ken Kesey Movie," *Rolling Stone*, 7 March 1970, p. 33.

4. Forman is interviewed by Tom Burke, "The Director's Approach—Two Views," *The New York Times*, 28 March 1976, section 2, p. 15.

5. See Gerald Mast, *A Short History of the Movies* (Indianapolis: Bobbs-Merrill, 1976), pp. 429–30.

6. Frank Kermode comments, "It is on the faces of Forman's actors that we observe the conflict," in *The London Times Literary Supplement*, 19 March 1976, p. 318.

7. Ken Kesey, *One Flew Over the Cuckoo's Nest* (New York: Signet, 1962), p. 270. All textual references are to this edition.

8. Ken Kesey, "Letter to Ken Babbs," in *Cuckoo's Nest*, ed. Pratt, pp. 338–39.

9. Silvano Arieti describes the schizophrenic's inclination to see abstractions in terms of their concrete manifestations in "Schizophrenia," in *American Handbook of Psychiatry*, ed. Arieti (New York: Basic Books, 1959), pp. 476–77.

10. Dale Wasserman, *One Flew Over the Cuckoo's Nest*, from the novel by Ken Kesey (New York: Samuel French, 1974), p. 6.

11. Forman, interviewed by Burke, p. 15.

12. Ibid.

13. *The News Journal* (Wilmington, Delaware), 17 January 1976, p. 22; orig. pub., *Los Angeles Times*, 16 January 1976.

14. David Denby, "An Adolescent Fantasy," *The New York Times*, 21 December 1975, section 2, p. 15.

15. Leslie Fiedler points out that Kesey reformulates "that most fundamental of American legends . . . [the] combat against white womanhood, portrayed as a frustrating and castrating power," in "Making it with a Little Shazam," *Book Week*, 2 August 1964, p. 10.

16. Michael Wood, "No, But I Read The Book," *The New York Review of Books*, 5 February 1976, p. 3.

17. In the novel, as a consequence of McMurphy's martyrdom, the men sign out of the hospital. However, in the movie, only Bromden leaves the hospital.

18. Kesey, interviewed by Goodwin, p. 23.

14
Control by
Camera:
Milos Forman as
Subjective
Narrator

■■■■■■■■■■■■■■■■■

George B. MacDonald

The film version of *One Flew Over the Cuckoo's Nest* is that rare adaptation which balances a respect for its literary source with a rich contribution of cinematic meanings. The picture establishes Czech director Milos Forman as a major director in contemporary American film-making.

Forman's role reaches far beyond the shaping of the actors' performances. It extends into the entire visual design and the literary structure of the film. Forman insisted that the film not be told from the first-person point of view of Bromden, for he wanted no single character's viewpoint to dominate in his adaptation. Partly as a result of Forman's intransigence in this matter, Kesey disassociated himself from the production, and two other writers, with Forman's help, wrote the final scenario.

Forman's elimination of the first-person viewpoint places Mc-Murphy and Nurse Ratched outside the subjective coloration of Bromden's projections. In the film McMurphy and the Nurse are equally

Originally published in *Lex et Scientia: The International Journal of Law and Science* 13: 1–2 (1977), pp. 81–86. Reprinted by permission.

matched and realistically ambivalent characters. On the whole, Forman's McMurphy is less admirable than Kesey's hero. The McMurphy
in the film is generous, spontaneous, and eager to teach what he
knows, but there is also much in him that is unheroic and even mean-
spirited. This is the McMurphy who complains to Dr. Spivey behind
the Nurse's back instead of confronting her directly; who repeatedly
punches Washington while the aide's body is pinioned by Bromden;
and who becomes maddened with infantile rage as he screams, "I
want that television set turned on—right now!" In a way Forman's
McMurphy simply has less character than Kesey's hero. This is evident in the two protagonists' attitudes toward work. Kesey's Mc-
Murphy is a brawny, Bunyanesque figure whose hands are calloused
from his days as a logger. He sees certain kinds of work as tests of
strength and forms of self-expression. Forman's McMurphy is just
the opposite. He is a shirker who looks on the state asylum as a "feed
farm." He allows his sanity to be questioned partly because the hospital which is observing him is also giving him a place to eat and
sleep.

Thanks partly to actress Louise Fletcher, the Nurse Ratched of the
film is a more admirable character than Kesey's nurse. Although in-
effective as a counsellor to the patients, she works hard at her job
and honestly believes that her "therapeutic" measures are what the
patients need. Perhaps not surprisingly, Forman's Nurse Ratched
partakes of the feminist politics of the seventies. We are never allowed
to forget that much of the exacting physical work of this hospital falls
on the shoulders of the nurses: Nurse Itsu may do the work in pre-
paring McMurphy for his electroshock, but it is the male doctor who
operates the control panel which sends the volts through his body.
Nurse Ratched's proximity to the three black aides indicates that her
officious personal identity is inseparable from her subjugated political
identity as a woman and a laborer. Even the Nurse's worst quality,
her consuming jealousy, is partly mitigated by the care she must
expend on a group of male patients who despise her and yet who
cannot live without her.

Forman is absolutely evenhanded in dealing with McMurphy and
Nurse Ratched. Each character is equally sympathetic and unsym-
pathetic. A kind of parodic Adam and Eve after the Fall, they are
locked in a deadly contest of "masculine" and "feminine" egos in
which each tries to humiliate the other in a series of progressively

more brutal agons. What the film makes clear is that McMurphy and the Nurse are equally dangerous. McMurphy, the male ego of exhibitionism, is solipsistic and socially irresponsible. Nurse Ratched, the feminine ego of bonded labor, is overly repressive and absorbed by form. Billy Bibbit, the androgynous child, is a symbolic externalization of what both McMurphy and Nurse Ratched have repressed and slain within themselves. Bibbit's suicide is an indictment of both McMurphy and the nurse, each of whom knows that Billy has attempted suicide in the past because of his sexual anxieties. The Nurse provides the immediate catalyst for the suicide when she invokes the name of Billy's mother after finding him in bed with Candy, but she is not the only one who pushes the boy to his death. McMurphy too is culpable in casually prescribing a sexual encounter for someone clearly not ready for such a "cure." The imagery of the film underscores the inappropriateness of McMurphy's therapy: Billy is pushed into the trysting room in a wheelchair, and the bed of love is festooned by leather straps used to belt down violent patients.

Forman has not made a work of pure realism out of *One Flew Over the Cuckoo's Nest*. Rather, he has turned Kesey's novelistic monodrama into a realistic allegory in which characters are both realistically and symbolically conceived. There is certainly a greater sense of history and time in Forman's film. The film opens around early autumn of 1963 and continues through the fall and early winter. Television newscasts keep us informed of such events of the day as the Birmingham Sunday bombing, the Christine Keeler saga, and the Cold War dramatics at the Berlin Wall. These events invoke images of racial conflict, scandal, and warfare. They are more appropriate to Forman's hospital than to Kesey's. Milos Forman has given us a film in which there is little hint of growth, development, or progress. Certainly Forman's eye is compassionate and full of comic appreciation, but it is an eye which rather pitilessly beholds a world gone mad, a world in which institutional rigidity makes it impossible for human beings to interact and learn from each other. Forman's is a gray film, suitable to the fall of 1963.

Rather than discuss further the film's departures from the novel, I would like to examine the ways in which Forman uses cinematic idioms as visual surrogates for elements in Kesey's novel. Two areas particularly rich in this respect are color and point of view. Through them Forman and the screenwriters convey the spirit of a literary work of art by using the techniques of the film maker's medium.

In Kesey's novel green and white play important roles in characterizing the ward. Patient uniforms and shower tiles are green; walls are white. McMurphy and Nurse Ratched, on the other hand, are associated with brighter, more dynamic colors. McMurphy's red hair suggests fire and heightened life just as the nurse's red-orange lipstick carries the weight of repressed anger. Milos Forman uses color imagery in a similar but even more pervasive way. When Forman picked one particular ward as his major set at the Oregon State Hospital, he had the walls painted in colors that would photograph as off-white, green, and a washed-out lemon-beige. The film creates a homogeneous color design by playing these watery shades into the liquid blues and yellow-greens of other parts of the hospital interior. Frequently all of these shades are set off by the richer, more saturated, seaweed greens of the trees and grass which are visible through the windows in the backgrounds of many of the interior shots. The pastel aquamarines evoke the medicinal and bodily fluids of a contemporary hospital. Forman immerses us so thoroughly within this watery chromatic haze that we sometimes feel as if we are drowning in a swamp of disinfectants and bedpan odors.

During the first part of the film Forman deliberately uses chromatic monotony to give the viewer a feeling of captivity within the ward's miasmic hospital colors. This helps to explain why we feel a sharp sense of release when the camera joins the inmates on their bus ride to the pier. The yellowish orange of the bus provides a change of color which is also a change of mood and meaning. One of the most lyrical shots in the film is the tableau shot in which the orange bus recklessly snakes through the green and beige exteriors of the hospital grounds. The meaning of the shot lies as much in the contrast of colors as it does in the movement of the bus and the promise it offers the inmates. Forman continues to work in orange in the next major sequence. The colorful orange life vests worn on the boat convey inner meaning through a chromatic alteration. It is a relief to see the patients out of their dull-colored, pajama-like uniforms. The color of the vests suggests the internal change of character which McMurphy briefly makes possible for the patients.

Like Kesey, Forman often uses bright colors to convey not simply freedom, but anger, danger, sexuality, and frustration. When, for

example, Nurse Ratched glares at the patients after their party, Forman places the camera so that the glowing red night light appears
just above her head, externalizing all the rage that is just beneath the
surface of her rigid countenance. Perhaps the most shattering use of
red lies in the thick film of blood which surrounds Billy as he lies
dead on the floor of the doctor's office. The meaning of Billy's death
is partly embodied in the colors of this shot, for the rich hue of the
blood clashes in a particularly ugly way with the pale green shade of
the floor. Somehow the clash between these two colors signifies the
lack of harmony which prevails at every level of this film. There is
no compromise between the wet greens and the hard orange-reds of
the *mise en scène*. The bright colors conflict sharply with the duller
tones. From color to idea, nothing is reconciled in Forman's *One Flew
Over the Cuckoo's Nest*.

The second area of cinematic expressiveness which needs attention in Forman's film is point of view. Forman may have upset Kesey
with his unwillingness to accept Bromden as the narrator and central
consciousness, but on the deepest level of cinematic expressiveness,
Forman has respected the *idea* of the subjective viewpoint which prevails in Kesey's novel. He universalizes the narrative consciousness
by using the "subjective camera" to give virtually all of the major
characters their own points of view in the film. Even more, through
his camera placements Forman reveals his own presence as the directorial architect of *One Flew Over the Cuckoo's Nest*. In this sense he
has not so much eliminated the first-person viewpoint of Bromden
as he has usurped it.

The term "subjective camera" usually refers to any shot in which
the camera photographs something through the eyes of one of the
characters in the dramatic situation. An example of this technique
from *One Flew Over the Cuckoo's Nest* is the low-angle shot of the
squirrel on top of the fence of the hospital yard as it appears to
McMurphy, who is standing below the fence looking up. Usually the
subjective camera indicates what a *character* sees in the film, but, in
a more encompassing way, it can present the director's viewpoint as
well. In Hitchcock's films, for example, both levels of the subjective
camera are present. Hitchcock identifies his camera with various of
the individual protagonists in his films at the same time that he identifies *himself* as the directorial presence with an encircling viewpoint
which watches over the characters as they watch one another.

In *One Flew Over the Cuckoo's Nest* Forman's use of the subjective camera is similar to Hitchcock's. Through this technique Forman reveals himself as the central consciousness of the film while at the same time "translating" the subjective consciousness of Kesey's novel into a cinematic idiom. The entire structure of the film is designed around variations of the subjective-camera technique. Let us look at two examples from the opening and closing framing passages of the film.

The first shot of the film is a fade-in on a mountainous landscape near dawn. The vista is without human life as the credits begin to appear on the screen. Suddenly a single flickering yellow-orange light appears at the left side of the screen. Then a second light appears at its side. These two headlights turn on and off in irregular rhythms as a car moves from left to right toward the center of the frame. Forman deliberately makes the lights flicker in a stylized manner so that the viewer will associate the car with something uncanny, magical, or at least subjectively conceived, for this is the car bringing Randle Patrick McMurphy to the mental hospital. As the car continues, Forman pans the camera to follow it out of the right side of the frame. At this moment Forman cuts from the rightward panning exterior shot to a leftward panning interior shot within Nurse Ratched's ward. In this second shot the camera pans and moves among the sleeping patients. The composition and editing of these first two shots suggest that McMurphy (the first shot) is in part a subjective projection emerging from the collective dream life of the patients (the second shot). Throughout the film Forman will use the subjective camera to suggest that many people see not the social world of fact but the projective mirror images of their own anxieties and expectations. The opening shots of the film presage these pervasive "mirror shots" by implying that McMurphy has a partly subjective existence in the minds of the helpless and sleeping patients, some of whom may be unconsciously anticipating and even projecting his arrival.

The concluding shots of the film are similarly subjective in design. In this sequence Bromden lifts the tub-room panel, throws it through a window, and disappears into the wilderness. The composition and the dramatic development of the film's last shot presents the exact reverse of the design of the first shot of the film. In the last shot Bromden runs away from the camera into the darkness of a mountainous landscape. As he slowly descends the slope of the hill, his entire body disappears from view until we are left with the same image which opened the film: a vista of New World nature wholly devoid of human civilization. On one level, Bromden's absorption by the land signifies a suicidal triumph of fantasy over reality; on another level, his escape to the wilderness is a subjective dream-fantasy in the minds of the hospital patients. Bromden escapes not during the day but at night when all the patients are asleep. At the moment he leaps out the window he is watched by the suddenly awakened Taber, whose cries of manic joy arouse a number of the other patients. There is the suggestion that Bromden's epic gesture lives as a fantasy image in the mind of the inarticulately helpless Taber, who may well have dreamt Bromden's superhuman feat of strength. The picture ends as it began: an image within an image.

All the individual characters in the film are defined by the subjective camera. None of them *sees* the world. Each merely *looks* at the world and tries to control it with the annulling and objectifying Look of Sartre's ocular assassin. When McMurphy talks with Dr. Spivey and when Nurse Ratched talks to the patients, the subjective camera usually cross-cuts between the various interlocutors to reveal that each individual is trying to "stare down" and degrade the other through the medium of a paranoid and aggressive Look.

Forman uses a number of techniques to deliver the viewer from the paranoid subjectivity of the individual characters of the dramatic situation. Frequently he plays the patients' subjective-camera views against the more universal subjective camera of the director. In these instances Forman develops a sequence by cross-cutting among the subjective views of the individual characters. Then he unexpectedly cuts back out of a scene in order to give us the artist's subjective viewpoint, which embraces a multitude of individual viewpoints. This technique is especially dramatic at the end of the fishing sequence. In the last shot of this sequence the camera leaps above the boat, where some of the patients are absorbed in catching a fish, to a helicopter-level shot of the boat. In this final shot of the fishing scene, the camera looks down with a rather merciless objectivity. What the camera sees is no longer a playful image of a group of people fishing, but a pathetic image of a boat going round in circles. The cut to the helicopter perspective is startling because the breadth of its compass makes the obsessiveness of the patients seem disturbingly private and self-centered. Here Forman has pulled us away from the insane subjectivity of the patients into the sane subjectivity of the artist.

There is also a Brechtian quality in the way Forman uses the directorial subjective camera. In a number of instances he breaks the viewer's emotional identification with the patients of this mental hospital by a shock technique in which the director functions in much the same way as a first-person narrator functions in telling a story. During one of the playground sequences, for example, Forman dramatically calls attention to the camera as the controller of the audience's sensibilities. In this scene McMurphy is trying to get the inmates to play a game of basketball. During the game, Martini, who cannot obey the rules of any game, receives the ball and, to our astonishment, throws it directly at the camera. The spectator inwardly ducks as the ball disappears below the lower border of the frame with a loud clanging noise. We do not understand what has happened until McMurphy cries out in frustration that Martini has thrown the ball into the fence. By this camera placement, Forman reminds the viewer that the director's camera is the central consciousness and the guiding viewpoint of this film. The ball flung at the lens is meant to wake us up to the fact that we are not the patients but the watchers of the patients. In the style of Brecht, Forman repeatedly catches us off-guard. Here he breaks our emotional rapport with the zany basketball game to warn us against becoming too involved with these characters, who are not "zany" at all. Forman wishes us not *to become* the people of this film but to learn something from their experience. The basketball, which all but bounces off the lens of the camera, keeps us alert to the much more serious "game" being played in and by this film.

A more audacious acknowledgment of the camera's power occurs during the boating excursion. After taking the boat from the pier, McMurphy turns the wheel over to Cheswick, who holds the wheel until he becomes anxious at being abandoned by the other inmates. They have become distracted by the love-making of McMurphy and Candy below. When Cheswick lets go of the wheel and heads below to join the others, Forman manipulates point of view in an unexpected manner. He fixes the camera upon the wildly spinning wheel. During this shot the audience feels as if it has been abandoned on the bridge of a boat which has no captain. Forman is again provoking the audience into realizing that we are as much at the mercy of the director as the passengers of a ship are dependent upon their captain. The camera's presence is acutely felt in this shot because Forman refuses to "rescue" the camera from its entrapment on a boat that is careening over the water under no control at all. As viewers we are made to feel somewhat like the helpless Cheswick as we watch the wheel spinning furiously in the foreground and feel the ocean swelling beneath us. Once our response has become this primitive, we realize that again Forman has caught us off guard. Again he has called our attention to the fact that the camera sets the boundaries of the audience's attention and that the *way* a screen narrative is told is just as important as what is being told. On a thematic level, this crazily subjective use of the camera is a serious warning to the audience, for it indicates how dangerous any society becomes which loses its principle of social organization. Forman is not an American primitive like Kesey. Nor is he an authoritarian East European social realist. He is an artist sensitive to the need for some kind of order in any social grouping. A society without cohesion is like a ship without a captain, or a camera without an artist behind it.

Forman's use of subjective-camera techniques thus creates in cinematic terms a world analogous to the subjective viewpoint of Chief Bromden in Kesey's *One Flew Over the Cuckoo's Nest*. In acknowledging both the dangers and the positive values of the subjective viewpoint, Forman's film is closer to Kesey's novel than one might think on a first viewing.

In imposing his own subjective viewpoint on the story, Forman altered somewhat Kesey's attitude toward insanity. Whereas Kesey sees the poetry in paranoia, Forman is more attentive to the destructiveness in all forms of mental unbalance. Kesey has more faith than Forman in the chances of the individual outside of social forms. Although there is some hope, even if rooted in fantasy, in the last page of Kesey's novel, there is nothing but a haunting image of self-annulment in the concluding frames of Forman's film.

It is possible, of course, to see Forman's film in a more optimistic light. Some viewers regard Bromden's use of speech and his climactic escape as indications of growth in at least one of the characters of the film. My own view is that to an extent Bromden is to McMurphy what McMurphy is to the rest of the patients: a fantasy screen. When Washington is beating up McMurphy, Forman uses a subjective camera to photograph Bromden's approach from the floor-level viewpoint of McMurphy. This camera angle tends to portray the Indian rescuer as at least partly a fantasy projection from the desperate McMurphy's point of view. There is a similar use of the subjective camera in the scene in which Bromden talks for the first time. Just before Bromden and McMurphy have their initial conversation, Forman photographs Bromden from McMurphy's viewpoint, suggesting that it is (only?) through McMurphy's eyes that Bromden becomes a speaking human being.

Forman's pessimism regarding the possibilities for human growth is emphatic in the last ensemble sequence in Nurse Ratched's ward. McMurphy is dead, and Bromden is gone, but relatively little has changed, except perhaps for the worse. Life on the ward ends as it began, with four of the patients playing cards at a table. Three of the players are the same ones who were playing at the beginning of the film: Harding, Cheswick, and Martini. The missing player is Billy Bibbit, the one patient who might have been saved. Replacing him at the table in this final scene is the irrevocably deranged Taber.

The film version of Kesey's novel is an extraordinary achievement. Its individual performances and its subtly orchestrated ensemble acting are remarkable. The screenplay is virtually without cliché. It manages the difficult task of consistently and imaginatively developing a large number of highly individualized characters. *One Flew Over the Cuckoo's Nest* is a brilliant adaptation of a literary work at the same time that it is an original and lasting achievement of cinema.

15
One Cuckoo
Flew Over
the Rest

◆◆◆◆◆◆◆◆◆◆◆◆◆

Dick DeBartolo

Mort Drucker

Originally published in *MAD Magazine*, July 1976, pp. 4–11. Reprinted by permission.
Copyright 1976, E.C. Publications, Inc., New York, NY 10022.

TROUBLE-MAKER AMONG THE INSANE! NO, IT'S NOT RALPH NADER! IT'S . . .

W OVER THE REST

WRITER: DICK DE BARTOLO

175

181

Bibliography

In compiling this bibliography, I have consulted the *MLA International Bibliography* for the years 1962–1989, along with the following:

Bischoff, Joan. "Views and Reviews: An Annotated Bibliography." *Lex et Scientia: The International Journal of Law and Science.* Perspectives on a Cuckoo's Nest: A Special Symposium Issue on Ken Kesey, edited by Peter G. Beidler and John W. Hunt. 13.1–2 (1977): 93–103.

Carnes, Bruce. "Selected Bibliography." In *Ken Kesey,* 47–50. Boise State University Western Writers Series, 12. Boise, ID: Boise State University, 1974.

Frank, Robert. "Ken Kesey." In *Fifty Western Writers: A Bio-Bibliographical Sourcebook,* edited by Fred Erisman and Richard Etulain, 246–56. Westport, CT: Greenwood Press, 1982.

Leeds, Barry H. "Bibliography." In *Ken Kesey,* 125–27. Modern Literature Series. New York: Ungar, 1981.

Tanner, Stephen L. "Selected Bibliography." In *Ken Kesey,* 150–54. Twayne's United States Authors Series. Boston: Twayne, 1983.

Weixlmann, Joseph. "Ken Kesey: A Bibliography." *Western American Literature* 10 (1975): 219–31.

———. "Selected Bibliography." In *One Flew Over the Cuckoo's Nest: Text and Criticism,* edited by John C. Pratt, 559–67. The Viking Critical Library. New York: Viking, 1976.

I have omitted interviews, biographical studies, reviews, articles in popular periodicals, unpublished doctoral dissertations, and treatments of Kesey's works other than *One Flew Over the Cuckoo's Nest.* I have also excluded the pieces reprinted in this volume. To the best of my knowledge, however, this bibliography is complete with respect to other scholarly articles and book chapters.

By necessity, the individual entries repeatedly refer to Kesey and to his books and characters. For the sake of simplicity, I have abbreviated those references as follows: Kesey is K, McMurphy is M, Chief Bromden is B, Nurse Ratched is R; *One Flew Over the Cuckoo's Nest* is *CN, Sometimes a Great Notion* is *SGN,* and *Kesey's Garage Sale* is *GS.*

Adams, Michael Vannoy. "Sex as Metaphor, Fantasy as Reality: An Imaginal

Re-Encounter With Ken Kesey and the Counter-Culture." *Indian Journal of American Studies* 15.2 (1985): 83–96.

Critic Robert Boyers is mistaken in terming *CN* an example of the "porno-political utopianism" of the 1960s, as such a categorization reduces the novel to the level of counter-revolutionary inauthenticity. What Boyers fails to understand is that *CN* is not—and does not purport to be—a realistic novel; rather, it's symbolic, metaphoric. "*CN* is . . . about the 'imaginal' construction of psychical . . . reality."

Allen, Mary. "Women of the Fabulators: Barth, Pynchon, Purdy, Kesey." In *The Necessary Blankness: Women in Major American Fiction of the Sixties*, 14–69. Urbana: University of Illinois, 1976.

The exaggeration inherent in fabulation allows for such vivid caricatures as R. Fabulation may not help us to know the intricate inner side of female characters, but it brings into focus many beliefs about women. R, for example, is the stereotyped castrating bitch, a symbol for all that is frightening or destructive about American matriarchy. Humorless, buxom but sexually repressed, malevolent, she is a central oedipal presence in the novel, yet her personality is never developed in any depth.

Atkinson, Michael. "One Flew Over the Fiction Course." *College Literature* 2.2 (1975): 120–27.

CN is an excellent choice for a fiction course, because it both engages students and affords the opportunity to study the various components of literary technique—point of view, setting, characterization, symbolism, et al.—as parts of one seamless whole.

Barsness, John A. "Ken Kesey: The Hero in Modern Dress." *Bulletin of the Rocky Mountain Modern Language Association* 23.1 (1969): 27–33. Reprinted in *One Flew Over the Cuckoo's Nest: Text and Criticism*, edited by John C. Pratt, 419–28. The Viking Critical Library. New York: Viking, 1976.

K's heroes—M in *CN*, Hank Stamper in *SGN*—are anachronisms: idealists, romantic individualists out of step with their unheroic age. Yet they remain heroes, embodying the roughhewn, Western myth of the hero typified by Mike Fink, Paul Bunyan, et al.

Baurecht, William C. "Separation, Initiation, and Return: Schizophrenic Episode in *One Flew Over the Cuckoo's Nest*." *Midwest Quarterly* 23.3 (1983): 279–93.

Through a repressed homoeroticism that "is necessary if men are to adopt polymorphous emotional lives," B is reborn a man after a prolonged schizophrenic episode.

Beards, Richard D. "Stereotyping in Modern American Fiction: Some Solitary Swedish Madmen." *Moderna Sprak* 63.4 (1969): 329–37.

Like Crane's "The Blue Hotel," Hemingway's "The Killers," and Porter's

Noon Wine, CN features a Swedish character (George Sorensen) who is an example of cultural stereotyping.

Beidler, Peter G. "From Rabbits to Men: Self-Reliance in the Cuckoo's Nest." *Lex et Scientia: The International Journal of Law and Science* 13.1–2 (1977): 56–59.

A basic theme of the novel is that of self-reliance, as defined by Emerson and Thoreau. Indeed, Thoreau can be seen as K's philosophical mentor. M is supremely self-reliant, hence his appeal. He is proof that the self-reliant can still exist in the modern world, yet his ultimate defeat lends the novel a tragic dimension.

Benert, Annette. "The Forces of Fear: Kesey's Anatomy of Insanity." *Lex et Scientia: The International Journal of Law and Science* 13.1–2 (1977): 22–26.

The novel is based on fear of women, fear of blacks, and fear of machines, and on the glorification of a "hero" who conquers these fears. But women, blacks, and machines have power in this novel only because they are given it, because, in the language of analytical psychology, it is projected onto them. Similarly, M's heroism is projected onto him by the other patients. B's salvation is that he is no longer dependent on fantasies and projections.

Billingsley, Ronald G., and James W. Palmer. "Milos Forman's *Cuckoo's Nest:* Reality Unredeemed." *Studies in the Humanities* 7.1 (1978): 14–18.

Although highly successful, the film version of *CN* lacks subtlety. Too obsessed with M's sexuality and too superficial in its portrayal of B, the movie avoids any mention of the Combine and omits the Christian symbolism of the book. And the fishing scene becomes simply crude comedy rather than an instance of psychological and spiritual transformation.

Bischoff, Joan. "'Everything Running Down': Ken Kesey's Vision of Imminent Entropy." *Lex et Scientia: The International Journal of Law and Science* 13.1–2 (1977): 65–69.

Although *CN* suggests that entropic forces can sometimes be held momentarily at bay, it remains a grim jeremiad, a prime example of the literature of entropy.

Blessing, Richard. "The Moving Target: Ken Kesey's Evolving Hero." *Journal of Popular Culture* 4.3 (1971): 615–27.

M—American folk hero, fertility god, primitive father, Christ figure—is the embodiment of energy. His rapid and relentless movement constitutes a triumph of freedom and motion over confinement and fixity.

Boardman, Michael M. "*One Flew Over the Cuckoo's Nest:* Rhetoric and Vision." *Journal of Narrative Technique* 9.3 (1979): 171–83.

In our uncertain age, literary tragedy may fail for want of a common philosophical ground between author and reader. But *CN* is a tragedy that succeeds, by lending significance to M's act of rebellion and self-sacrifice. And it is the book's tragic exigencies—its "local rhetoric"—rather than any objective justification, that have generated charges of racism and sexism.

Boyd, George M. "Parables of Costly Grace: Flannery O'Connor and Ken Kesey." *Theology Today* 29.3 (1972): 161–71.

K's *CN* and O'Connor's "The Artificial Nigger" exemplify the contrasting conceptions of sin and grace represented by traditional (O'Connor) and radical (K) theology. Superficially, *CN* is a parable of resistance to a dehumanizing techno-bureaucratic society, but on a deeper level it is more. Though K would never be mistaken for a "Christian writer," *CN* is the preeminent literary paradigm of redemption. K obviously intends M as a secular Christ figure.

Boyers, Robert. "Attitudes Toward Sex in American 'High Culture.'" *Annals of the American Academy of Political and Social Sciences* (March 1968): 36–52. Reprinted in part as "Porno-Politics" in *One Flew Over the Cuckoo's Nest: Text and Criticism*, edited by John C. Pratt, 435–41. The Viking Critical Library. New York: Viking, 1976.

K's solution to the problem of authoritarian repressiveness takes two forms: laughter and sensuality. Based on the reactionary myth of male supremacy, the novel is an example of "porno politics"—an idea popular among Utopian socialists who, frustrated by more conventional avenues to social change, claim that uninhibited sexuality can effect a perfectly harmonious society.

Brady, Ruth H. "Kesey's *One Flew Over the Cuckoo's Nest*." *Explicator* 31.6 (1973): 41.

A close examination of K's use of symbolism reveals that B does not achieve true freedom by escaping the hospital ward, for the forces of the Combine are everywhere. He "has escaped from one cage into a larger one."

Bross, Addison C. "Art and Ideology: Kesey's Approach to Fiction." *Lex et Scientia: The International Journal of Law and Science* 13.1–2 (1977): 60–64.

CN is an "inauthentic" fiction, because it is too dependent on an intrusive (if popular) ideology: the idea that a repressive establishment is in command of our world.

Carnes, Bruce. *Ken Kesey*. Western Writers Series, 12. Boise, ID: Boise State University, 1974.

A Westerner, K is heir to the tradition of cowboy and frontier-hero literature, which makes itself felt in his characters and his themes. His are the themes of American fiction generally, the stuff of Adamism. In *CN*, K presents the Utopian view that heroism can be achieved and the enemy defeated through direct, individual action. *CN* has much in common with the southwestern tradition of American humor, the tall tale, and the comic book and television Western, not to mention Christian parable.

Crump, G. B. "D. H. Lawrence and the Immediate Present: Kurt Vonnegut, Jr., Ken Kesey, and Wright Morris." *D. H. Lawrence Review* 10.2 (1977): 103–41.

Vonnegut, Morris, and K sometimes evince the romantic habit of mind, which finds expression in an anti-technology, pro-Nature stance. In this and in other ways their approaches to their material are often strikingly similar to Lawrence's.

DeBellis, Jack. "Alone No More: Dualisms in American Literary Thought." *Lex et Scientia: The International Journal of Law and Science* 13.1–2 (1977): 70–73.

In various ways, *CN* draws upon Melville, Twain, James, Steinbeck, Salinger, Nabakov, Kerouac, Bellow, Emerson, Whitman, Hawthorne, Faulkner, Mailer, Crane, Dreiser, Hemingway, Cooper, and Baldwin.

———. "Facing Things Honestly: McMurphy's Conversion." *Lex et Scientia: The International Journal of Law and Science* 13.1–2 (1977): 11–13.

The most important meanings in the novel pivot on M's change of heart. By abandoning self-protection in favor of self-sacrifice, M not only resurrects B, but also transcends his own ego and preserves his own integrity.

Doxey, William S. "Kesey's *One Flew Over the Cuckoo's Nest.*" *Explicator* 32.4 (1973): 32.

The novel's title derives from a children's counting-rhyme, and the expression "cuckoo's nest" functions on several levels.

Fick, Thomas H. "The Hipster, the Hero, and the Psychic Frontier in *One Flew Over the Cuckoo's Nest.*" *Rocky Mountain Review of Language and Literature* 43.1–2 (1989): 19–34.

Much of our greatest literature is based on the conflict between wilderness and civilization—i.e., between Hip and Square. Like the frontier hero, the modern-day hipster rebels against the established order, but also battles largely for the sake of conflict itself. Women in *CN* also reflect the regimentation-versus-freedom opposition, embodying the polarities of both Hip and Square. "*CN* is a powerful novel which effectively translates into contemporary terms the enduring American concern with a freedom found only in—or between—irreconcilable oppositions."

Fiedler, Leslie. "The Higher Sentimentality." In *The Return of the Vanishing American*, 169–87. New York: Stein and Day, 1968. Reprinted in part in *One Flew Over the Cuckoo's Nest: Text and Criticism*, edited by John C. Pratt, 169–87. The Viking Critical Library. New York: Viking, 1976.

CN is an archetypal Western, embodying the old fable of the white outcast and the noble red man joined together against home and mother, the female world of civilization. Its sentimentality, its melodrama, and its cartoon-like nature are part of the method of its madness, its underlying suggestion that madness is fundamental.

Fifer, Elizabeth. "From Tragicomedy to Melodrama: The Novel Onstage." *Lex et Scientia: The International Journal of Law and Science* 13.1–2 (1977): 75–80. Despite the casting of Kirk Douglas as M, Dale Wasserman's stage version of *CN* was a commercial failure, perhaps because Wasserman created melodrama out of the tragicomedy by relying on some of the novel's weakest effects (stereotyped characters, exaggeration, predictable and frequent confrontation) and a blend of superficial dramatic techniques.

Flora, Joseph M. "Westering and Women: A Thematic Study of Kesey's *One Flew Over the Cuckoo's Nest* and Fisher's *Mountain Man*." *Heritage of Kansas* 10 (1977): 3–14.
K's *CN* and Vardis Fisher's *Mountain Man* have both been made into films (the latter as *Jeremiah Johnson*) that glorify the spirit of the free man. But while K portrays women as an obstacle to male freedom and fulfillment, Fisher depicts women as essential to male growth and fulfillment. Hence Fisher's treatment is more adult.

Forrey, Robert. "Ken Kesey's Psychopathic Savior: A Rejoinder." *Modern Fiction Studies* 21.2 (1975): 222–30.
Critic Terence Martin is incorrect in his favorable estimate of *CN*, which is actually conservative, sexist, and lowbrow. Although a favorite of the 1960s counterculture, *CN* is really a throwback to the he-man bromides and overt Christ symbolism of Hemingway and Steinbeck.

Foster, John W. "Hustling to Some Purpose: Kesey's *One Flew Over the Cuckoo's Nest*." *Western American Literature* 9.2 (1974): 115–30.
K as author of *CN* is like a poolroom hustler, combining gamesmanship and inspired lyricism, innocent vision and inspired cunning—much like his protagonist, M. Indeed, this is a basic theme: the spiritual or hierophanic vision versus the practical and secular. M is a Christ figure, a folk hero, somewhere between character and caricature. Ultimately, though, the book is serious in intent.

Gallagher, Edward J. "From Folded Hands to Clenched Fists: Kesey and Science Fiction." *Lex et Scientia: The International Journal of Law and Science* 13.1–2 (1977): 45–50.
CN embodies several themes central to science fiction, principally the idea of people being manipulated, controlled, and dehumanized by the machine. In this sense the novel can be compared to many science fiction films of its period, and to such fictions as Forster's "The Machine Stops," Huxley's *Brave New World*, Harlan Ellison's "I Have No Mouth, and I Must Scream," et al.

Gilbert, Basil. "*One Flew Over the Cuckoo's Nest*: Madhouse or Microcosm?"

Meanjin 35.3 (1976): 292–99.

K's mental institution is more than a simple sanitorium. One of the morals of the novel is that it can also be seen as a most Kafkaesque institution, where conformity to society's norms is enforced. The film, like the novel, raises a number of probing questions.

Graybeal, David M. "On Finding the Cuckoo's Nest." *Christian Century,* 4 August 1976: 688–89.

M's story is a re-creation of Christ's, reinforced by numerous symbolic parallels. The enthusiastic response of the film's audiences attests to a collective, if subconscious, recognition of the correspondence.

Handy, William J. "Chief Bromden: Kesey's Existentialist Hero." *North Dakota Quarterly* 48.4 (1986): 72–82.

It's unfortunate that the film version of *CN* is better known than the book, because the film focuses too exclusively on M. The novel is really about the "viewpoint character," B. In portraying B, K is closer to "the consciousness novels of Faulkner and Joyce" than to the novel of external event. B—isolated, victimized by society's mechanisms, but ultimately choosing life—is an existential character, and K's vision is that of the existentialist rather than the realist.

Hauck, Richard Boyd. "The Comic Christ and the Modern Reader." *College English* 31.5 (1970): 498–506.

Because of twentieth-century agnosticism and skepticism, authors often present Christ figures in a somewhat parodic or comic way, while still attempting to convey a serious message. *CN* is one novel that typifies this approach, as are Steinbeck's *Grapes of Wrath,* Faulkner's *Light in August* and *As I Lay Dying,* and Barth's *Giles Goat-Boy.*

Hays, Peter L. "Kesey's *One Flew Over the Cuckoo's Nest* and Dante's *La Vita Nuova.*" *Explicator* 46.4 (1988): 49–50.

The passage in which M claims to have experienced sexual intercourse when "around ten" years old is based upon Dante's statement that he first saw Beatrice at roughly the same age.

Heatherington, Madelon E. "Romance Without Women: The Sterile Fiction of the American West." *Georgia Review* 33.3 (1979): 643–56.

Like all Western fiction, *CN* perpetuates a puerile, escapist fantasy in which females exist only as predictable stereotypes, either purely good or utterly bad. The basic dynamics of romance are aborted in Western novels, preventing the genre from reaching its full potential. Hence the cardboard characterization of R in *CN* weakens the mythic confrontation between her and M.

Herrenkohl, Ellen. "Regaining Freedom: Sanity in Insane Places." *Lex et Scientia: The International Journal of Law and Science* 13.1–2 (1977): 42–44.

The novel contains two dramas: M's struggle against external forces, and

B's inner struggle against himself. Through M's struggle, B is able to succeed in recapturing a sense of personal reality.

Hipkiss, Robert A. *Jack Kerouac: Prophet of the New Romanticism.* Lawrence, KS: Regents, 1976.

Like Kerouac and Thomas Wolfe, K creates heroes who exult in sensation and physicality. K's M draws upon comic strip heroes such as Superman and Captain Marvel to become a sort of secular activist Fisher King. Thus K's M is more successful than Kerouac's heroes, because he influences the lives of others, imparting a traditional American message of Emersonian/Whitmanesque rugged individualism.

Horst, Leslie. "Bitches, Twitches, and Eunuchs: Sex-Role Failure and Caricature." *Lex et Scientia: The International Journal of Law and Science* 13.1–2 (1977): 14–17.

Although in other respects an excellent novel, CN is a bit retrograde because it promotes a demeaning view of women, a most constricted view of masculinity, and an unconstructive view of the relationship between the sexes.

Horton, Andrew S. "Ken Kesey, John Updike and the Lone Ranger." *Journal of Popular Culture* 8.3 (1974): 570–78. Reprinted in *Seasoned Authors for a New Season: The Search for Standards in Popular Writing,* edited by Louis Filler, 83–90. Bowling Green, Ohio: Popular, 1980.

K in CN and Updike in *Rabit Redux* use the Lone Ranger myth as a means to focus on contemporary issues and to suggest alternatives to what they see as the chaos of the present. K inverts the myth; Tonto is saved by the Lone Ranger.

Huffman, James R. "The Cuckoo Clocks in Kesey's Nest." *Modern Language Studies* 7.1 (1977): 62–73.

The connection of the word "cuckoo" with insanity, making "cuckoo's nest" an insane asylum, is well-known. The word is also readily associated with clocks, and K makes much of this association as well, alluding repeatedly to clocks and chronological time.

Knapp, James F. "Tangled in the Language of the Past: Ken Kesey and Cultural Revolution." *Midwest Quarterly* 19.4 (1978): 398–412.

Although K's novels are thought to be countercultural, really they're quite conservative, espousing traditional—if contradictory—ideals: individualism and interdependence. K would create a new community based on self-sacrifice and mutual dependency. Yet his community would include only the elect. There was a kind of siege mentality about much of the counterculture; hence K's attraction to the idea of the beleagured warrior-Christ.

Larson, Janet. "Stories Sacred and Profane: Narrative in *One Flew Over the Cuckoo's Nest.*" *Religion and Literature* 16.2 (Summer 1984): 25–42.

CN employs a story form "that tends toward truth, that works toward liberation for the hearers . . . [and is] both dialectical and dialogical. . . . While *CN* is not a Christian novel . . . its dynamic narrative structure models the possibility for genuine transcendence in this world and liberates its readers through a dialectic of myth and parable."

Leeds, Barry H. "Theme and Technique in *One Flew Over the Cuckoo's Nest.*" *Connecticut Review* 7.2 (1974): 35–50. Reprinted as *"One Flew Over the Cuckoo's Nest:* 'It's True Even If It Didn't Happen,'" in Leeds, *Ken Kesey,* 13–43. Modern Literature Series. New York: Ungar, 1981.

CN rejects hypocritical bureaucracy, and celebrates healthy sexuality and the exuberant expression of individual identity. The narrator, B, is crucial to K's method. While M declines, B ascends, as a transfer of power occurs between the two. B's narration is a highly credible integration of prose style and metaphorical patterns: castration, hands, animals, and Christ imagery. Despite its excellence, however, *CN* is not K's best book; *SGN* is.

Lena, Hugh F. and Bruce London. "An Introduction to Sociology through Fiction Using Kesey's *One Flew Over the Cuckoo's Nest.*" *Teaching Sociology* 6.2 (1979): 123–31.

The use of literary selections can enliven introductory sociology courses. *CN* is a particularly apt choice for such a strategy, because it addresses a wide range of issues and concepts typically covered in introductory sociology.

Loeb, Roger C. "Machines, Mops, and Medicaments: Therapy in the Cuckoo's Nest." *Lex et Scientia: The International Journal of Law and Science* 13.1–2 (1977): 38–41.

In its depiction of the mental hospital, *CN* is a mixture of accuracy and distortion; the latter tends to override and invalidate the former. Many mental hospitals do stress obedience and subservience, and an occasional R may even exist, but such abuses are the exception rather than the norm.

MacDonald, George B. "The Rules of the Game: Milos Forman's American Allegory." *Lex et Scientia: The International Journal of Law and Science* 13.1–2 (1977): 87–91.

Milos Forman's film version of *CN* uses image patterns (nationalistic symbols, sports, mirrors, et al.) to create a highly symbolic allegory that presents M as a quixotic anachronism.

Madden, Fred. "Sanity and Responsibility: Big Chief as Narrator and Executioner." *Modern Fiction Studies* 32.2 (1986): 203–17.

B, rather than M, is the central character, as he progresses toward sanity. B is increasingly able to strengthen his self-reliance, while M loses his, becoming increasingly controlled by the other patients on the ward. If

M is made a sacrificial victim by the ward, B is made its executioner. Indeed, B's murder of M is his last act as a member of the group, and the "confessional" narrative is driven by B's sense of guilt.

Malin, Irving. "Ken Kesey, *One Flew Over the Cuckoo's Nest.*" *Critique* 5.2 (1962): 81–84. Reprinted in *One Flew Over the Cuckoo's Nest: Text and Criticism*, edited by John C. Pratt, 429–34. The Viking Critical Library. New York: Viking, 1976.

CN is an example of New American Gothic, dealing with a microcosm to elucidate the larger societal picture. K uses a great deal of striking, highly effective imagery to convey his almost manic condemnation of society.

Maxwell, Richard D. "A New Viewpoint: The Invisible Narrator." *Claflin College Review* 2.1 (1977): 24–29.

Like Ralph Ellison in *Invisible Man*, K in CN has used the device of an "invisible" narrator. Since B is ignored by other characters, he has greater objectivity, more access to information, and more freedom of movement, becoming almost an omniscient narrator.

McCreadie, Marsha. "*One Flew Over the Cuckoo's Nest:* Some Reasons for One Happy Adaptation." *Literature and Film Quarterly* 5.2 (1977): 125–31.

Although there are structural differences between the novel and the film, and some alterations in the characters, the momentum and spirit of the original remain. Principal strengths of the film are fine casting, and the impact of M. The film avoids surrealistic touches, because viewers unfamiliar with the novel would find them difficult to accept.

McGrath, Michael J. Gargas. "Kesey and Vonnegut: The Critique of Liberal Democracy in Contemporary Literature." In *The Artist and Political Vision*, edited by Benjamin R. Barber and McGrath, 363–83. New Brunswick, NJ: Transition, 1982.

K's CN allegorically emphasizes the outmoded nature of Jeffersonian ideals of individualism in contemporary society. The cuckoo's nest has much in common with the slums of urban America, the patients with the poor in American society, the hospital bureaucracy with bureaucracies everywhere. The two protagonists who vie for control of public values— R and M—represent distinct, antithetical perspectives on public action in modern life. R is a model of bureaucratic efficiency, while M is the heroic rebel against the established order.

Messenger, Christian K. "Play, Sacrifice, Performance: Kesey and Coover." In *Sport and the Spirit of Play in Contemporary American Fiction*, 125–53. New York: Columbia, 1990.

CN focuses on "the power of play," as M continuously uses games— basketball, monopoly, poker, and other forms of ritual sport—to energize his ward-mates. "Kesey has proven that play can be a powerful element in neutralizing or suspending the normally oppressive relationships be-tween authority and the dominated." Similarly, K's *SGN* and Robert Coover's *The Public Burning* are much concerned with "control through performance."

Mills, Nicolaus. "Ken Kesey and the Politics of Laughter." *Centennial Review* 16.1 (1972): 82–90.

The world of *CN* is like that of *Brave New World* or *1984*. The asylum is but a microcosmic part of the larger Combine. M's rebellion—K's "politics of laughter"—is a comedy that demonstrates the weakness of such a world. But M is not a Christ figure; his laughter arises from a belief in the sufficiency of worldliness. He sees his punishment as a parody of Christ's.

Morey-Gaines, Ann-Janine. "Of Menace and Men: The Sexual Tensions of the American Frontier Metaphor." *Soundings* 64.2 (1981): 132–49.

Because the "wild West" is defined in part by its repudiation of tradi-tionally female principles, the "gunfighter hero" stands in opposition to women. Thus M's struggles in *CN* are primordially sexual. Yet K stacks the deck, reducing complex cultural issues to simplistic formulae based on exclusively male prerogatives and dependent on violence.

Oleksy, Elzbieta. "Kesey and Pynchon: A Trip to the Wasteland." *Revue Belge de Philologie et d'Histoire* 64.3 (1986): 520–31.

Like Pynchon's *The Crying of Lot 49*, K's *CN* is a modern American ro-mance that draws upon certain long-established traditions. The waste-land theme, the Fisher King and Grail Knight motifs—all are present, as is the agon-pathos/anagnorisis structure. Both novels typify "the tradi-tion of allegory and the imperishable romance."

Palumbo, Donald. "Kesey's and Forman's *One Flew Over the Cuckoo's Nest*: The Metamorphosis of Metamorphoses as Novel Becomes Film." *College English Association Critic* 45.2 (1983): 25–32.

Like Kafka's *Metamorphosis*, *CN* uses the death/rebirth archetype, yet this motif is far more central to the novel than to the film. Since the movie does not center on B, the book's psychological depth is lost, as is K's extensive system of Christian and other symbolism. The film retains the novel's comedy, but not its more significant implications.

Pearson, Carol Sue Havemann. "The Cowboy Saint and the Indian Poet: The Comic Hero in Kesey's *One Flew Over the Cuckoo's Nest*." *Studies in American Humor* 1.2 (1974): 91–98.

Critic Raymond Olderman is mistaken in claiming that *CN* is based on the Fisher King myth. Really the novel uses a different fertility myth: the romantic myth of the king, the hero, and the fool (with M as fool and B as king and hero).

Phillips, Guler Paran. "Ken Kesey and the Language of Prose Fiction." *Lin-*

guistics in Literature 1.3 (1976): 23–38.

By the end of the novel, B's choice of nonstandard English is deliberate, a reflection of his newfound identity.

Porter, M. Gilbert. "The Plucky Love Song of Chief 'Broom' Bromden: Poetry from Fragments." In *The Art of Grit: Ken Kesey's Fiction*, 7–35. Literary Frontiers. Columbia: University of Missouri, 1982.

In K's view the real enemy is the failure of self-reliance caused by fear. The men have submitted to institutional forces, acquiescing in their own victimization. M pits his will to live against their will to die. Ironically, their lives are granted only in exchange for his death, a messianic bargain attended by tragicomic Christian symbolism. B's change into a courageous, self-reliant defender of others testifies to the validity of M's heroic message. The novel's most important artistic features are K's handling of poetic first-person point of view and a prose use of synecdoche; the novel's dominant images are of laughter, hands, and faces.

Roach, Bruce V. "'One Flew Over the Mere.'" *Old English Newsletter* 14.2 (1981): 18–19.

In certain respects, *Beowulf* and the film of *CN* are similar. For example, both depict "individual-versus-institution" conflict.

Roberts, William H. "Narrative Technique in *One Flew Over the Cuckoo's Nest*." *Notes on Contemporary Literature* 9.4 (1979): 11–12.

K gives credibility to the novel's narrative voice—especially in the last four paragraphs of the first chapter—through a careful mixture of ambiguity, imagery, grammatical deviation, and flashback.

Rosenman, John B. "Kesey's *One Flew Over the Cuckoo's Nest*." *Explicator* 36.1 (1977): 23.

While B's vote enables the patients to achieve the necessary majority of twenty-one votes in their attempt to watch the televised World Series, the number twenty-one also suggests the card game of blackjack, as well as B's "coming of age."

Rosenwein, Robert. "Of Beats and Beasts: Power and the Individual in the Cuckoo's Nest." *Lex et Scientia: The International Journal of Law and Science* 13.1–2 (1977): 51–55.

The novel's political/social view derives from the Beat Generation of the 1950s. But M's activism is more akin to that of the 1960s. Since M himself is ultimately defeated, however, K is suggesting the limitations of that style. Currently there is no clear path to finding balance between individual integrity and interdependence.

Scally, Thomas. "Origin and Authority: An Analysis of the Relation Between Anonymity and Authorship in Ken Kesey's *One Flew Over the Cuckoo's Nest*." *Dalhousie Review* 62.3 (1982): 355–73.

In *CN* "there is a recognized incongruity between the true and the factual;

the Chief's account is strictly phenomenal, its truth intrinsic to shape, and its sense unmeasured. . . . The imaginative as experienced, as inhabited by truth prior to judgment, is the frame for a derived factuality. In this way, before one even has a world, one already has the truth about it, for the truth is more enclosure than enclosed."

Searles, George J. "McMurphy's Tattoos in Kesey's *One Flew Over the Cuckoo's Nest.*" *Notes on Modern American Literature* 1.3 (1977): 24.

M's tattoos not only reinforce his characterization as a battler, but also prefigure his eventual fate as a sacrificial victim.

Schopf, William. "Blindfolded and Backwards: Promethean and Bemushroomed Heroism in *One Flew Over the Cuckoo's Nest* and *Catch-22.*" *Bulletin of the Rocky Mountain Modern Language Association* 26.3 (1972): 89–97.

Like Heller's *Catch-22, CN* is representative of the 1960s, depicting social alienation and instability. But neither book advocates a Promethean defiance of authority; actually they encourage us to circumvent confrontation. While Heller's Yossarian and K's M eventually lose, Orr and B succeed, by virtue of unattachment and disengagement.

Shaw, Patrick W. "The American West as Satiric Territory: Kesey's *One Flew Over the Cuckoo's Nest* and Berger's *Little Big Man.*" *Studies in Contemporary Satire* 10 (1983): 1–8.

Judged as satire, *CN* fails because the narrator is overshadowed by M, who is clearly an authorial projection. K is guilty of sentimental oversimplification, because he fails to maintain the distancing necessary to good satire. In *Little Big Man*, on the other hand, Thomas Berger expertly manages the ironic point of view to deflate the same frontier myths that figure so pervasively in K's novel.

Sherman, W. D. "The Novels of Ken Kesey." *Journal of American Studies* 5.2 (1971): 185–96.

"In his two novels . . . Kesey has described that sense of the disintegration and death and ultimate rebirth of the ego which lies at the heart of the LSD 'trip.' Both books are literary metaphors for psychedelic experiences."

Sherwood, Terry G. "*One Flew Over the Cuckoo's Nest* and the Comic Strip." *Critique* 13.1 (1971): 96–109. Reprinted in *One Flew Over the Cuckoo's Nest: Text and Criticism*, edited by John C. Pratt, 382–96. The Viking Critical Library. New York: Viking, 1976.

K uses the popular culture—particularly the Lone Ranger comic strip—to reinforce his somewhat simplistic moral vision of a clear-cut opposition between good and evil, between natural man and society, between an older mode of existence honoring masculine physicality and a modern, machine-oriented culture inimical to it.

Singer, Barnet. "Outsider Versus Insider: Malamud's and Kesey's Pacific

Northwest." *South Dakota Review* 13.4 (1975): 127–44.

Although Malamud (in *A New Life*) is an outsider to the Pacific Northwest and K an insider, both are regional writers. "Kesey, as insider . . . goes in an opposite direction from Malamud. . . . Kesey's province is a freedom that needs regaining. Malamud . . . urges the province outward." Each, however, is subversive, which regional writers must be.

Slater, Thomas J. "*One Flew Over the Cuckoo's Nest:* A Tale of Two Decades." In *Film and Literature: A Comparative Approach to Adaptation,* edited by Wendell Aycock and Michael Schoenecke, 45–58. Lubbock: Texas Tech University, 1988.

Although M appears to be heroic, really he is just as flawed as R and Harding, because he too is motivated primarily by the desire for power. Really B is the hero, as he—not M—"exemplifies K's message of individual responsibility" and thereby embodies the popular beliefs of the 1970s. Forman conveys this partly by alterations in the plot, but also by use of the "subjective-camera" technique.

Stein, Howard F. "The Cuckoo's Nest, the Banality of Evil and the Psychopath as Hero." *Journal of American Culture* 2.4 (1980): 635–45.

The evil protrayed in the film is not a consciously monstrous evil, but the evil of routine ordinariness. The evil of the ward takes the form of "a rationalized incivility" in the service of an obsessive-compulsive need for order. Hence any disruption of the norm—even a disruption that will ultimately "improve" the patients—is seen as a problem, punishable. The film depicts the dialectic of overcontrol (R) and anarchy (M). And although the film encourages us to "side with" M, "to take sides . . . is to perpetuate the pathology." Therefore the film oversimplifies the moral issues, and "exploits our passions rather than giving us insight."

Stone, Edward. "*Cuckoo's Nest* and *Moby-Dick.*" *Melville Society Extracts* 38 (1979): 11–12.

There are many parallels between *CN* and Melville's *Moby-Dick,* as M (like Ahab) is a monomaniac who engages in a fatal struggle from which he knows he is powerless to desist.

Stone, Edward. "Straws for the Cuckoo's Nest." *Journal of Popular Culture* 10.1 (1976): 199–202.

In *CN* there are echoes of Melville, Twain, and especially Faulkner, whom K has discussed in *GS,* and with whom he shares a tragic vision.

Sutherland, Janet R. "A Defense of Ken Kesey's *One Flew Over the Cuckoo's Nest.*" *English Journal* 61.1 (1972): 28–31.

"Ken Kesey's *One Flew Over the Cuckoo's Nest* is not obscene, racist, or immoral, although it does contain language and scenes which by common taste would be so considered."

Tanner, Stephen L. "One Flew Over the Cuckoo's Nest." In *Ken Kesey,* 18–

51. Twayne's United States Authors Series, 444. Boston: Twayne, 1983. Broadly popular and exceptionally teachable, *CN* features a "hero of event" (M) and a "hero of consciousness" (B). Their story revolves around familar themes and archetypes: the sacrificial savior, death and rebirth, the search for the father, American folk myths, popular culture, nature versus the machine, etc. The novel is divided into four parallel parts; at the beginning of each, R is ascendant, and at the end M is ascendant. Dominant symbols include laughter, hands, faces, Christian imagery, and size as a metaphor for strength. Despite the novel's artistry and its emphasis upon the traditional American virtue of self-reliance, it has sometimes been attacked for its portrayals of blacks and women.

———. "Salvation Through Laughter: Ken Kesey & the Cuckoo's Nest." *South West Review* 58.2 (1973): 125–37.

Although experimental in tone, *CN* is conventional in technique; the novel's real merit lies in its tight organization and skillful imagery, particularly "nature-versus-machine" symbols. The novel is built on the archetypal struggle between good and evil, and the idea of a sacrificial hero, as K makes playful use of Christian symbolism.

Tanner, Tony. "Edge City (Ken Kesey)." In *City of Words: American Fiction 1950–1970*, 372–92. New York: Harper & Row, 1971.

CN is deliberately schematic, like a cartoon strip. M acts out one of the most enduring and simple of American fantasies: the will to total freedom, total bravery, total independence. R is a projection of the nightmare reversal of that fantasy: total control. What is unusual is the brilliant way in which K has created the paranoid vision of a schizophrenic in the narrative voice, which owes much to William S. Burroughs.

Valčić, Sonja. "Kesey and Bellow—The World of Madness and Inarticulateness." In *Cross-Cultural Studies: American, Canadian and European Literatures 1945–1985*, edited by Mirko Jurak, 115–19. Ljubljana, Yugoslavia: University of Ljubljana, 1988.

Much American literature is ambivalent about the social contract. Hence, speech itself—the vehicle by which cultural precepts are perpetuated—is called into question. Some writers actually create inarticulate characters whose silence is a metaphor for "the traditional American fear of boundaries and communal impositions." K's B is an example of this, as are several characters in Bellow and Faulkner.

Valentine, Virginia. "Kesey's *One Flew Over the Cuckoo's Nest*." *Explicator* 41.1 (1982): 58–59.

Textual evidence suggests that B escapes the mental hospital only to find death. Both M and B are in effect "crucified," much like Christ and St. Peter.

Van der Wilt, Koos. "Kesey's *One Flew Over the Cuckoo's Nest*." *Explicator* 40.3

(1982): 60–61.

Some critics maintain that K uses comic-strip motifs in *CN*. Harding, for example, is based on the skinny character in old comic-book cartoon advertisements for body-building courses.

Vardaman, James M. "Invisible Indian: Chief Bromden of Ken Kesey's *One Flew Over the Cuckoo's Nest*." *Journal of the English Institute* 11 (1980): 43–63.

CN embodies the time-honored American literary theme of the individual versus society. As both narrator and participant, B plays an important role in the novel. Like the narrator of Ellison's *Invisible Man*, he learns that "invisibility" has its advantages. Believed to be deaf and dumb, he is an ideal narrator because he is privy to much that would otherwise be kept hidden from him. As participant, B personifies K's belief that the individual can stand up to society.

Waldmeir, Joseph J. "Two Novelists of the Absurd: Heller and Kesey." *Wisconsin Studies in Contemporary Literature* 5 (1964): 192–204. Reprinted in *One Flew Over the Cuckoo's Nest: Text and Criticism*, edited by John C. Pratt, 401–18. The Viking Critical Library. New York: Viking, 1976.

Only two American novels since World War II—Heller's *Catch-22* and K's *CN*—can truly be considered absurdist. But *Catch-22* is a failure, while *CN* is a success, thanks to K's novelistic integrity and the book's tightly controlled design.

Wallace, Ronald. "What Laughter Can Do: Ken Kesey's *One Flew Over the Cuckoo's Nest*." In *The Last Laugh: Form and Affirmation in the Contemporary American Comic Novel*, 90–114. Columbia: University of Missouri, 1979.

CN has been criticized as racist and sexist, but we must recognize that the novel is a comedy, not a romance, and that B, not M, is the hero. B's development toward a comic understanding parallels M's development from eiron to Lord of Misrule to sacrificial redeemer.

Waxler, Robert. "The Trap of Chief Bromden's Truth in Kesey's *One Flew Over the Cuckoo's Nest*." *Notes on Modern American Literature* 4.3 (1980): 20.

Although some critics read the novel's conclusion positively, arguing for B's rebirth, really he remains "invisible," for he "has no place to go."

Widmer, Kingsley. "*One Flew Over the Cuckoo's Nest* (Ken Kesey)." Audiotape. Twentieth Century America Novel series, cassette #115. Deland, FL: Everett/Edwards, 1975.

Our interest in *CN* is as much sociopolitical as literary, for the novel dramatizes a whole period's collective attitude. Like Salinger's *Catcher in the Rye* in the 1950s, this lively and provocative work embodies the moral stance of its decade. Similarly, Kesey himself commands attention not only as a writer, but also as pacesetter of the psychedelic counter-culture—an almost legendary figure whose exploits are chronicled in Tom

Wolfe's *The Electric Kool-Aid Acid Test*. Kesey's life, as well as his book, is a protest against bureaucratized passivity and robotic uniformity. Yet the novel is weakened by its melodramatic treatment of the female characters (all are portrayed as dominating witches or submissive whores) and by the unlikelihood of protagonist M's transformation from amoral picaro into tragic Christian martyr.

Widner, Kingsley. "The Perplexities of Protest: Mailer, Kesey and the American 'Sixties.'" *Sphinx* 3.4 (1981): 28–38.

See Widmer, "The Post-Modernist Art of Protest."

———. "The Post-Modernist Art of Protest: Kesey and Mailer as American Expressions of Rebellion." *Centennial Review* 19.3 (1975): 121–35.

Despite their differences, K's *CN* and Mailer's *Armies of the Night* bracket some of the rebellious social-aesthetic responses of the American 1960s. Both books are by novelists indebted in sensibility and technique to literary modernism, but who consciously attempted to supercede the aesthetic in commitment to a rebellious social role. While *CN* is the better book, both are deeply flawed, because of the limitations of forced art, which make them half-protests, half-novels.

Wiener, Gary A. "From Huck to Holden to Bromden: The Nonconformist in *One Flew Over the Cuckoo's Nest*." *Studies in the Humanities* 7.2 (1979): 21–26.

In several respects—for example, the use of an emotionally childlike narrator in conflict with technocratic society—*CN* is akin to both Salinger's *Catcher in the Rye* and Twain's *Huckleberry Finn*.

Wills, Arthur. "The Doctor and the Flounder: Psychoanalysis and *One Flew Over the Cuckoo's Nest*." *Studies in the Humanities*. 5.1 (1976): 19–25.

The crucial fishing scene operates on three symbolic levels. It reinforces the idea that homogenized society must be escaped. In addition, the fishing trip possesses a religious dimension. And thirdly, there is a complex psychological undercurrent, as the fish the patients catch represent their inner difficulties now brought into the open.

Yonce, Margaret J. "*One Flew Over the Cuckoo's Nest* and the Myth of the Fisher King." In *The Power of Myth in Literature and Film*, edited by Victor Carrabino, 92–102. Tallahassee: University of Florida, 1980.

K draws upon the Fisher King myth to invest *CN* with numerous parallels. B is the Fisher King, M is the Grail Knight, the hospital—and, by extension, society—is the wasteland, etc.

Contributors

PETER G. BEIDLER is the Lucy G. Moses Distinguished Professor of English at Lehigh University. His most recent scholarly book, *Ghosts, Demons, and Henry James: "The Turn of the Screw" at the Turn of the Century,* was published by the University of Missouri Press in 1989. His articles have appeared in *PMLA, Modern Fiction Studies, Chaucer Review, American Indian Quarterly,* and many other journals. In 1983 he was named Professor of the Year by the Council for Advancement and Support of Education in Washington, D.C.

DICK DEBARTOLO and MORT DRUCKER have collaborated on numerous parodies for *MAD* magazine and are recognized worldwide as leading figures in the field of popular satire.

JOHN W. HUNT has returned to teaching English at Lehigh University after serving fifteen years as Dean of Lehigh's Arts and Science College. The major focus of his publications has been on Faulkner, although he has also dealt with many recent writers as well. He is the recipient of two teaching awards, including the E. Harris Harbison Award for Distinguished Teaching.

JEROME KLINKOWITZ is Professor of English at the University of Northern Iowa and is the author of more than thirty books on contemporary culture, including *Literary Disruptions, The Life of Fiction, Kurt Vonnegut,* and *The New American Novel of Manners.*

DON KUNZ is Professor of English at the University of Rhode Island, where he has served as Director of Graduate Studies in English and Director of the University Honors Program. Professor Kunz teaches courses in British and American literature and film studies. He has published satire, narrative, and poetry as well as essays on British drama, American fiction, American film, and pedagogy. His work has appeared in *Confrontation, Critique, Forum for Honors, Literature/Film Quarterly, Studies in American Fiction, War, Literature, and the Arts, Western American Literature, Vietnam Generation,* and other small magazines.

GEORGE B. MACDONALD is Assistant to the Dean of Academic Affairs at Massasoit Community College (Brockton, Massachusetts). He is writing a study of the American film studio during the Roosevelt and Cold War periods.

TERENCE MARTIN is a Distinguished Professor of English at Indiana University. He is the author of *The Instructed Vision: Scottish Common Sense Philosophy and the Origins of American Fiction*, and *Nathaniel Hawthorne*, and is an associate editor of the *Columbia Literary History of the United States*.

RICHARD D. MAXWELL teaches in the Dade County (Florida) public school system. He has also taught at Hamline University, North Carolina Central University, Clarkson University, and Claflin College. In addition to the article reprinted here, he has published on Kesey in *The Claflin Review*.

ELIZABETH McMAHAN, professor of English at Illinois State University, has published *A Crash Course in Composition*, now in its fourth edition. She has coauthored with Susan Day *The Writer's Rhetoric and Handbook*, and *The Writer's Resource: Readings for Composition*. With Susan Day and Robert Funk she has co-authored four textbooks for writers. Her articles have appeared in *Modern Fiction Studies*, the *CEA Critic*, the *English Journal*, *Illinois English Bulletin*, and *Teaching English in the Two-Year College*.

RAYMOND M. OLDERMAN left his position as a tenured associate professor of English at the University of Wisconsin-Madison in 1980. His book *Beyond the Waste Land* was published by Yale University Press in 1972. His articles have appeared in *The Iowa Review*, *Fiction International*, and *Contemporary Literature*.

ROBERT E. ROSENWEIN is Professor of Social Relations at Lehigh University. He is coauthor (with Carol Barner-Barry) of *Psychological Perspectives on Politics* (Prentice-Hall, 1986) and co-editor (with James Maddux, Cal Stoltenberg and Mark Leary) of *Social Processes in Counseling and Psychotherapy* (Springer-Verlag, 1987). His articles have appeared in *The Journal of Nonverbal Behavior*, *The Journal of Politics and the Life Sciences*, *Contemporary Social Psychology*, *Personality and Social Psychology Bulletin*, and elsewhere. He is currently editor of the journal *Contemporary Social Psychology*.

ELAINE B. SAFER is professor of English at the University of Delaware. She has published *The Contemporary American Comic Epic: The Novels of Barth, Pynchon, Gaddis, and Kesey* (Wayne State University Press, 1988). She has published essays on the contemporary novel in such journals and books as *Studies in the Novel*, *Critique*, *Studies in American Humor*, *Renascence*, *Critical Essays on Thomas Pynchon*, and *The American Writer and the University*. In fall, 1990, she was a Fulbright lecturer in American Literature at Universitié Jean-Moulin Lyon III, France.

The late RUTH SULLIVAN held a Ph.D. from Tufts University. At the time her *Cuckoo's Nest* essay was published, she was teaching at Northeastern University. She also placed articles in *Studies in Romanticism* and *Studies in American Fiction*.

The late JAMES R. TUNNELL was the pastor of Chapelwood United Methodist Church in Lake Jackson, Texas. He held a doctorate in theology from Princeton University.

BRUCE E. WALLIS is associate professor of English at the University of Victoria (British Columbia). His book *Byron: the Critical Voice* was published in 1973. His articles have appeared in the *University of Toronto Quarterly, Victorian Newsletter, Studies in Short Fiction,* and elsewhere.

Index